Classroom Killers? Hallway Hostages?

KENNETH S. TRUMP

Classroom Killers? Hallway Hostages?

How Schools Can Prevent and Manage School Crises

CORWIN PRESS, INC.
A Sage Publications Company
Thousand Oaks, California

For information:

CORWIN
PRESS

Corwin Press, Inc.
A Sage Publications Company
2455 Teller Road
Thousand Oaks, California 91320
E-mail: order@corwinpress.com

Sage Publications Ltd.
6 Bonhill Street
London EC2A 4PU
United Kingdom

Sage Publications India Pvt. Ltd.
M-32 Market
Greater Kailash I
New Delhi 110 048 India

Printed in the United States of America

Library of Congress Cataloging-in-Publication Data

Trump, Kenneth S.
 Classroom killers? Hallway hostages?: How schools can prevent and manage school crises / by Kenneth S. Trump.
   p. cm.
 Includes bibliographical references (   ).
 ISBN 0-7619-7510-1 (cloth: alk. paper)
 ISBN 0-7619-7511-X (pbk.: alk. paper)
 1. School crisis management—United States. 2. School violence—United States—Prevention. 3. Schools—Security measures—United States. I. Title.
  LB2866.5 .T78 2000   00-008379

This book is printed on acid-free paper.

00   01   02   03   04   05   10   9   8   7   6   5   4   3   2   1

Corwin Editorial Assistant: Julia Parnell
Production Editor: Denise Santoyo
Editorial Assistant: Victoria Cheng
Typesetter/Designer: Barbara Burkholder
Cover Designer: Tracy E. Miller

Contents

Disclaimer and Legal Notices

Although the author has attempted to ensure the accuracy of information contained herein, we do not warrant that it is complete or accurate. The author and publisher do not assume, and hereby specifically disclaim, any liability to any person or entity with respect to any loss or damage alleged to have been caused by any error or omission, as well as for the use or misuse of strategies described, herein.

All specific individual concerns should always be directed toward qualified professionals in those areas on an individual basis. Nothing in this book is provided as a substitute for legal, medical, police, or other professional advice or intervention.

Information contained is this book is not applicable in states or localities with laws, ordinances, regulations, and/or other legal restrictions that specifically prohibit any suggestions or recommendations made in this book.

Foreword

first became acquainted with Kenneth S. Trump in December 1997 after my observance of a tragedy at the high school I had attended. My wife and children are also graduates of Heath High School in West Paducah, Kentucky. On December 1, 1997, a young freshman student had opened fire on the morning prayer group, killing three of my youngest daughter's fellow students and wounding five more. Mr. Trump, President and Chief Executive Officer of National School Safety and Security Services, knew from news accounts that I was serving as vice chairman of the McCracken County Public Schools Board of Education, and, as soon as he heard of our tragedy, he sent me his first book, *Practical School Security: Basic Guidelines for Safe and Secure Schools* (1998). He included a handwritten expression of his sympathy and offered his book to assist our board as we began to embark on territory that we had never had reason to think much about: school safety and security.

The advice and guidance in Mr. Trump's first book proved to be a valuable tool because of his ability to convey a very complicated subject in practical terms. Although his first book focused on security measures that definitely make our schools safer, he knows the subject matter well enough to know that there is no 100% foolproof method for guaranteeing complete safety in our schools.

Due in part to our tragedy and many others since, Mr. Trump has now published *Classroom Killers? Hallway Hostages? How Schools Can Prevent and Manage School Crises*. I believe that this book is a must for every school district in our nation because I now know that no one is immune to the violence in today's world. Having experienced the unthinkable, the one thing I would urge all school leaders to do is to prepare. Not only must school districts implement more stringent security measures, but they also must be well trained in handling a crisis, were one to occur. In our situation, we learned a tremendous amount, but ideally we should have been prepared ahead of time—and we were not.

My involvement in school safety and security has led me to meet many so-called experts, but, when I started having discussions with Mr. Trump, it became obvious that he truly knew the business. I was also fortunate enough in April 1998 to attend one of his school safety workshops in New Orleans, Louisiana, at the National School Board Conference; there, I witnessed his ability firsthand. His knowledge of and expertise in virtually every facet of the subject has been a tremendous asset to me. I want to emphasize again that all districts should realize a tragedy *can* occur in their school system, and preparing ahead of time is the key to minimizing the many problems you may encounter. This book can be a wonderful training tool for our teachers and administrators, but, as with any tool, it is of very little value unless it is used.

Although no one has yet pinpointed the exact causes of these acts of violence, Mr. Trump's experience goes a long way in dealing with the prevention, as well as the aftermath, of a crisis, and both are of extreme importance. The tragedy of lost innocent lives is the worst thing I have ever witnessed, and the prevention of its recurrence is worth the investment of all the time and money imaginable. The key to prevention is awareness and readiness, and Mr. Trump most definitely provides both in the following pages.

I sincerely hope that you not only read this book, but also take time to study it, to absorb the information it contains, and then immediately to start implementing its recommended measures. There is a lot to know about the violence that has, unfortunately, become so prevalent in today's society, and this book contains much of that knowledge. Although I hope that you take the time to read this book, my most sincere wish is that you never have to put into action most of what you learn.

—Randy Wright
Vice Chairman
McCracken County Public Schools Board of Education
Paducah, Kentucky

Preface

Classroom killers and hallway hostages. Candy, my lovely wife and business partner, was the first of several respected individuals in my life who wasted absolutely no time in warning me that these words in my book title could easily drive potential readers away from this book. "Even though I know where you are coming from," she advised, "some people may think that it is overly dramatic."

Knowing that Candy is my first and foremost link to the creative side of the human brain (a part sometimes AWOL from my head), I began processing her concern in hotels, airports, and even while writing the heart of the manuscript itself. I increasingly wondered if I would risk losing some educators, who would be afraid to be seen with this book on their desk. In fact, I was actually at the point of tossing around new titles as I was put- ting the finishing touches on the manuscript.

And then it happened. I received word that an inner-city high school assistant principal had been shot in the leg after a confrontation with an armed student at the exact time that I was finishing my book on school crisis incidents. My determination to keep the title suddenly gained new strength.

This determination was strengthened further after I shared information on this most recent shooting with Chuck Hibbert, a friend and colleague with whom I regularly exchange messages on current events in the field. Chuck, the security coordinator for Wayne Township schools in the Indianapolis area, replied to my message of the shooting by noting that, unfortunately, because it had occurred in an inner-city area and because nobody had died, it would probably not make the national headlines on the evening news.

As usual, Chuck's point was well taken. He had echoed a message that I have been driving home more and more over the past year: If a school violence incident does not involve multiple suspects, multiple fatalities, multiple firearms, or a rural or suburban school, it is no longer news in our country.

Although I do not believe that school violence should dominate the headlines each day, I do firmly believe that educators, like most other Americans, tend to forget about the importance of security and crisis preparedness until there is a high-profile incident or series of incidents. I also believe that the education community has sugarcoated negative issues for the sake of public relations for so many years that, until recently, the typical school culture has been one where good or pretty things are portrayed as the norm, and where the bad and the ugly have been "phoo-phooed" (my term) to the point that too many adults working in schools have forgotten that we live in a society filled with negatives, obstacles, and ugly things. Those who do still remember this point are either labeled cynics and alarmists, or they simply are outnumbered and pushed to the side as "retirees waiting to happen."

And so, the words *classroom killers and hallway hostages* remain on the cover to remind readers that violence is ugly, that crisis situations cannot be dismissed, and that we need to accept that these situations are a part of our society—even of our schools. Stories on school violence should not dominate the headlines and the tabloids every week, and educators should not become cynics. School officials should, however, recognize reality, and prepare to prevent and manage crisis incidents in our schools until we actually live in the Utopian society that some people in our schools actually believe already exists.

Can we prevent every incident of school violence? Certainly not. But we can take steps to reduce the risks of these incidents occurring and to prepare to manage those that we cannot prevent, hence the second and most important portion of the book title, *How Schools Can Prevent and Manage School Crises.*

It quickly became evident during the writing of my first book, *Practical School Security: Basic Guidelines for Safe and Secure Schools* (1998), that the topic of school crisis preparedness warranted its own separate publication. The paucity of information on school crisis preparedness from a professional school security perspective reinforced this need. This book serves as a starting point for filling these gaps.

Part I of this book places everyone on the same playing field in terms of framing school crisis incidents. Chapter 1 describes how the high-profile school violence incidents of 1997-1999, especially the tragedy in April 1999 at Columbine High School, plunged America into a range of reactions, including paranoia, the political exploitation of school safety issues, and public relations campaigns focusing on school safety. Furthermore, school safety was the focal point of discussion in almost all education circles. Chapters 2 through 4 sift through these dynamics to identify what practical lessons were learned from these crises, how school security threats continue to shift, and whether or not we can really catch on to the so-called early warning signs to prevent similar incidents from occurring in the future. Part II moves the reader from awareness of the need to act to action itself. How should educators manage student threats of violence? How can school administrators reduce risks and prepare for crisis situations without creating prisonlike environments? These and related questions are answered in Chapters 5 and 6.

The third section of the book, Chapters 7 through 9, details the critical considerations educators and support staff, emergency service officials, parents, and others must consider in developing an effective school crisis preparedness planning process and related guidelines. In addition to providing specific suggestions for school crisis guidelines, these chapters should raise many questions that readers must answer on their own because of the unique nature of their schools, districts, and communities. Effective school crisis preparedness is a process, not a single event, and this book is intended to serve as a tool to facilitate the process—not as a fill-in-the-blanks template that all schools across the nation can complete simply to say that they have a plan.

It is here, in Part III, that readers will learn the basic steps of the crisis planning process, and will see what priorities to consider in the first half hour of a crisis, what to do before emergency service personnel arrive, and how to help them, as well as students and staff, when emergency personnel do arrive on the scene. Readers will also learn how to deal with the post-crisis crisis: the overwhelming arrival of parents and media following a crisis incident, as well as the psychological, community, political, and legal issues that will likely dominate the lives of crisis managers for months, and probably even years, after the crisis incident itself is over.

Part IV looks at how state and federal government agencies, along with colleges and others, can help our educators with their crisis planning efforts in a practical, meaningful way. These pages should leave readers from these arenas with clear answers to the question so often heard after a high-profile school crisis incident occurs in our nation: "What can we do?"

School administrators, teachers, support staff (such as bus drivers, secretaries, and custodians, to name a few), counselors and psychologists, law enforcement and other emergency service providers, policymakers, parents, the media, and students can benefit from reading this book. I also believe that our colleges and universities must step up to the plate to better prepare our educators for the stark realities of the classrooms and hallways. This book, along with my first book on school security, can serve as a text to introduce school personnel to these new issues and strategies. Finally, the many politicians who intend to propose legislation and funding to address school safety should read this book at least once to develop a more detailed understanding of how they can really help, in meaningful and beneficial ways, those people out on the front lines with our children.

The question we must ask is not whether the recent school violence tragedies are a wake-up call, but whether or not we will simply continue to hit the snooze button and go back to sleep without doing all we can to improve school security and crisis preparedness. I truly hope that this book provides enough information for everyone to get an early start on these issues.

Readers interested in sharing their thoughts or in learning more about what we do at National School Safety and Security Services may visit our website, *www.schoolsecurity.org*, and then e-mail me at *kentrump@aol.com*.

Acknowledgments

After working daily on school security and crisis issues for the past 15 years, and having "matured" in recent years to an age where one begins to look at the present and future somewhat differently, I now recognize more how much I treasure certain people who have touched my life in ways that they may not even know. The list begins with my wife, Candy; my parents, Bob and Fran Trump; and my father- and mother-in-law, Carlos and Nora Rodriguez. They all represent the true spirit of love, caring, and support to the utmost degree, and their support has enabled me to withstand the greatest of life's challenges and crises—including the completion of this book!

Thanks also to Michelle Rodriguez for her office support services and for her willingness to listen, regardless of whether or not she really wants to do so, and to Ana Rodriguez for simply being Ana. I must also acknowledge the three "top dogs" in our family: Brownie, Ginger, and Ally. Anyone who does not believe in "pet-assisted therapy" need only visit our place to appreciate the role of animals in calming humans in a crisis.

My appreciation goes out to those who supported me when, for some strange reason, I insisted on entering the school security field over 15 years ago. Judy Clark, Jane Engle, Nona Hamilton, Kathy Higham, Alice Koporc, Denny and Bobbie Rawson, and many others at the Cleveland Board of Education top that list. Likewise, those who stood with me through many circumstances when it was not popular to do so also deserve my acknowledgments: Jim Zielinski, John Fechko, Bill Gant, Ron Huff, Mary Lentz, Linda Schmidt, Steve Sroka, Kevin Zimmer, members of the original Cleveland BOE Youth Gang Unit, and members of the Cleveland Police Gang Unit, led by Wayne Torok, Dave Swan, and Bob Kumazec. A special thanks must also be sent to Ralph Witherspoon of Witherspoon Security Consulting in Cleveland for being a true friend and colleague who has left open his door and his mind to me throughout my venture as a full-time professional security consultant.

It is equally important to acknowledge a few professional colleagues for their outstanding leadership and support. Under the guidance of State Superintendent Suellen Reed, Indiana Department of Education staff members Cathy Danyluk and Steve Davis, along with their safe school team members from local school districts, including Chuck Hibbert, Duane Hodgin, Al Kasper, and Jack Martin, and First Sergeant Joe Wainscott of the Indiana State Police have been true leaders in taking school security and crisis preparedness leadership to a higher level. Indiana Governor Frank O'Bannon and his education assistant, Larry Grau, took the lead through their creation and advocacy for the passage of safe schools legislation, which has provided resources to Indiana schools for enhancing their school safety, security, and crisis preparedness. They are all commended for their dedicated and bipartisan leadership on these issues.

My thanks are also extended to Randy Wright, current board vice chairman for the McCracken County School District, who took a strong leadership role at the time of the violence crisis at Heath High School in West Paducah, Kentucky. Randy's thoughtful comments in the foreword, along with his continued friendship since the time of his crisis, have been much appreciated. His strength and leadership illustrates how our elected leaders can make a difference in school safety and crisis preparedness.

I would be remiss if I did not give special recognition to my friend and colleague Curt Lavarello, Executive Director of the National Association of School Resource Officers. Curt is one of the true giants in our profession who really cares about his profession and his fellow professionals. His integrity, character, and commitment are assets not only to NASRO, a truly professional association in itself, but also to a field where egos, dollar signs, and personal and political agendas often take priority over the real issues of school safety and crisis preparedness.

Last, but certainly not least, my thanks and appreciation to the staff at Corwin Press for their relentless support in making my first book a success and my second book a reality. Alice Foster deserves an award for her patience and guidance, while Suzanne Luce, Linda Miller, Vicky Ramirez, and the rest of the crew all deserve medals for their constant support with requests, promotions, and sales. Gracia Alkema's leadership and support is evident throughout this team!

I sincerely believe that all of the individuals above join me in dedicating this book to the children and school staff who have lost their lives and who have been injured as a result of school violence. No person should have to be courageous simply to go to school to learn, to teach, or to provide the necessary support services for those who wish to do so. Let us hope that no one else will ever have to face the violence that so many have had to face in recent years.

—Ken Trump

About the Author

Kenneth S. Trump is President and CEO of National School Safety and Security Services, a Cleveland-based national consulting firm specializing in school security and crisis preparedness training, assessments, and related consulting. He served over seven years with the Division of Safety and Security for the Cleveland Public Schools, the last three as founding supervisor of its Youth Gang Unit. Ken then served as assistant director of a federally funded gang project in three southwestern Cleveland suburbs, where he was also director of security for the ninth largest Ohio public school system. In January 1997, he expanded his very active part-time training and consulting business into a full-time operation that has included work in over 30 states and in Canada.

Ken chairs the K-12 Security Subcommittee of the Educational Institutions Security Standing Committee of the American Society for Industrial Security. He is cofounder of the Midwest Gang Investigators Association's Ohio chapter, has served on the board of the National Association of School Safety and Law Enforcement Officers, and is a member of the International Association of Professional Security Consultants.

He has consulted and trained for organizations nationwide, including the National School Boards Association, the National Governors Association, the FBI National Academy, the U.S. Department of Justice, the Parent Resource Institute for Drug Education (PRIDE), the Public Risk Management Association, and hundreds of schools, local, state, and national agencies, and professional organizations.

In addition to a BA in the social service field, Ken has a Master of Public Administration from Cleveland State University. He has received extensive specialized training in school safety and crisis preparedness, gangs, and related juvenile crime prevention issues.

Ken is author of the 1998 book, *Practical School Security: Basic Guidelines for Safe and Secure Schools*, which generated personal responses from President Clinton, Attorney General Reno, and numerous national authorities.

He is quoted extensively in the national media, including on Good Morning America, ABC World News Tonight, CBS This Morning, NBC Nightly News, CNBC, MSNBC, CNN, CNN Headline News, Fox News, USA Today, *Time Magazine*, and the Associated Press. In May 1999, he testified before the U.S. Senate Committee on Health, Education, Labor, and Pensions at its school safety hearing.

Ken is very happily married to Candy Rodriguez-Trump. They live in Cleveland, Ohio, with their three "children": Brownie and Ginger (two Pomeranians), and Ally (a Chow, German Shepherd, and northern-breed mixed puppy).

PART

I

Framing the Issues

Tragic school violence incidents rocked the United States in the late 1990s and sent Americans scurrying to understand why these incidents occurred, how to prevent future incidents, and how to prepare to better manage those incidents that cannot be prevented.

If anything positive came out of these tragedies, it is unquestionably the placement of school safety at the top of the educational agenda and discussion list for school and community leaders nationwide. The flip side of this, however, is that the increased attention to school safety also generated political debates and agendas, an explosion of overnight experts and opportunists, and often distorted responses to safety issues due to the rhetoric and slanted views spouted by those with alternative motives and agendas.

This book is not designed to recant statistics or the details of the various tragic incidents. The sad reality is that there will probably be even more such incidents between the time this book is written and the time that it hits the bookshelves. We can, however, learn from the past, and Chapters 1 through 4 help do so by sorting out the political, administrative, and other dynamics so that readers can get to the bottom line of what really has been learned from these violent incidents.

1

From Paranoia to "Politricks" and PR Campaigns

America Responds to Tragedy

The question is not whether these incidents of school shootings and bombings are wake-up calls. The real question is whether or not we will keep hitting the snooze button and going back to sleep again instead of maintaining balanced, proactive school security and crisis preparedness measures in all of our schools.

A series of school shootings and violent acts rattled the American education community between 1997 and 1999. These tragedies took place in cities including, but not limited to: Pearl, Mississippi; West Paducah, Kentucky; Jonesboro, Arkansas; Edinboro, Pennsylvania; and Jefferson County, Colorado. For the first time in history, educators, public safety officials, and other youth service professionals nationwide were forced to struggle with questions not only about why these incidents occurred but also about what was being done to prevent future incidents and, in the worst-case scenario, to prepare for managing those that could not be prevented.

The facts of the various incidents were covered in detail in various news media outlets, professional publications, and comparable sources. In fact, the news coverage of these incidents was so extensive that it brought a great deal of focus to the issue of media sensationalism, and raised questions as to how much coverage is actually adequate. Rather than recounting the horrifying details of each incident yet another time, it suffices to say that the shootings, bombings, and related violence associated with each of these occurrences triggered the need for a closer analysis of how schools have handled security and crisis preparedness in the past, and how they need to rethink and refine for the future.

Decades of Neglect Hit Home

Traditional Approaches to School Safety

Educators have historically addressed school safety from disciplinary, prevention, and intervention perspectives. Principals have handled violations of school rules with detentions, suspensions, and expulsions. Many have only called the police for the most serious of incidents.

Teachers and counselors have instructed violence prevention curricula of all flavors, as have an increasing number of police officers. Conflict resolution, peer mediation, counseling, psychological support programs, and similar intervention programs have been created to mitigate potential violent circumstances and individual behaviors. Psychologists and counselors are mobilized on short notice for student and staff deaths, suicides, and related concerns.

School officials develop and promote a variety of themes for improving school climate and culture. They use mission statements, logos, themes, promotional messages, signs, public address announcements, newsletters, posters, signs, contests, giveaways, and many other approaches to drive home messages about the importance of practicing respect, accepting diversity, resolving conflicts peaceably, and displaying related nonviolent behaviors. In fact, improving school climate is the first approach cited by most administrators when asked how they are addressing school safety, and it is even a factor in many performance evaluations for educators.

There is no doubt that firm, fair, and consistent discipline is an essential ingredient for keeping order in schools, and that a school's climate and culture, just like that of a corporation, sets a major tone for how individual behavior plays out in that environment each day. Likewise, prevention and intervention programs are essential components for shaping and reshaping current and future behaviors of youth. Yet even with all of these measures, violence continues to take place in our schools. Why?

The Missing Links

Many school officials have done an excellent job addressing the prevention, intervention, and discipline end of the school safety spectrum. However, far too many have failed to address the security and crisis preparedness perspectives as well, leaving their schools vulnerable to those immediate security threats that are outside the realm of traditional discipline, prevention, and intervention strategies. Although they have recognized the need to shape youth behavior in the long term, which is the amount of time needed for most prevention and intervention programs to have a true impact on behavior changes, they have failed to take steps beyond traditional discipline to deal with the here-and-now security threat issues.

Logic and common sense dictate that a school's afternoon violence prevention curriculum and peer mediation program will not be very successful if there is a morning multiple shooting in the school hallway. Ironically, although many educators have thought that they were doing everything possible to improve school safety through these types of programs, they have failed to take even the most basic security measures needed to provide a more secure environment for the delivery of these and other educational programs! School officials have been so focused on long-term behavioral changes to effect school safety that they have neglected to take steps to reduce the very short-term threats that jeopardize the potential maximum impact of their longer term programs.

These steps are centered on proactive, balanced security procedures and crisis preparedness planning. But if it is this simple, then why did we not figure this out years ago and move on to prevent the tragedies of recent years?

Traditional School Safety Politics

In my first book, *Practical School Security: Basic Guidelines for Safe and Secure Schools* (Trump, 1998), I stressed that "politricks"—political tricks—have unquestionably been the biggest obstacle to having professional school security programs in many schools throughout recent years. Denial, image concerns, and the underreporting of school crimes for the purposes of protecting the school reputation and image have driven school administrators in the opposite direction of best practices in school security and crisis preparedness. Fear of adverse media attention, parent complaints, and being perceived by members of the school community as a poor manager have historically taken precedence over proactive security measures in many schools, creating and testing crisis guidelines and similar necessary measures for protecting students, staff, and facilities in the here and now.

For example, reducing the number of doors open from the outside is one of the most basic security measures that any organization can take to reduce security risks. This practice is common at many, if not all, government offices, private corporations, and even fast food restaurants. Yet until recently, many school administrators have skirted the issue because too many parents and staff would complain about the added inconveniences created by such measures.

Controlling access is one of the most simple and basic forms of reducing security risks. It does not cost a great deal of money to close a door with a panic bar so that people on the inside can get out in an emergency, but people on the outside cannot simply walk into the schools as they wish. Until recently, however, we have failed to implement even this most rudimentary practice in the majority of our nation's schools, only to be surprised when someone states that schools have poor security practices!

Think about the last time you went to a fast food chain. Most likely, some of the doors, at least those to the employee work areas, were closed from the outside. You were also probably greeted rather promptly by an employee with "Good morning. May I help you?"

Now think about your average local elementary school. Chances are good not only that there are a number of open doors, but also that no conscious effort has been made in the past to secure at least some of them. Even if some effort has been made, the odds are favorable that when you walked inside, you could go almost anywhere you chose and nobody would ever challenge your presence with an inquiry or even a "Good morning. May I help you?"

Why, then, should we be surprised by incidents of school violence when we have historically protected hamburgers in fast food chains better than we have our children? And, although it is sad to say, the reality is that we have typically failed to protect our children better because issues of convenience, denial, image, and "politricks" have taken priority over security.

A Twisted Philosophy?

A number of school administrators and academicians have argued that the approach to school safety is simply a matter of philosophy. Prevention and school climate are typically at one end of the continuum, with security and crisis preparedness at the other end. Philosophically and politically, the debate has then centered around more prevention *or* tighter security.

Although an either/or debate might make an interesting philosophical or political debate, it does not make good sense from a safety perspective. Why should the question focus on more prevention *or* tighter security? Should it not be an argument for more prevention *and* tighter security?

Related arguments for more prevention are often as flawed as the broader argument itself. For example, many educators, academicians, and politicians automatically equate school security with high-ticket equipment items and increased manpower. As explained in Chapter 6, professional school security programs rest on a foundation of policies and procedures, training, professional assessments, and crisis preparedness planning, and, although manpower or equipment may fall into the picture at some point in time, they do not solely represent the concept of school security either by themselves or collectively.

An additional point of frustration centers on the perception of security as being reactive or punitive. To the contrary, an effective school security program will actually be preventive in nature. Until educators begin to view security and crisis preparedness as the first line of prevention, and not as last-resort punitive measures, schools will never reap the benefits of a full, comprehensive school security program.

Columbine Reshapes Thinking

The series of school shootings in the 1997-1998 school year raised eyebrows, discussions, and various forms of action on security and crisis preparedness like never before in our history. But the shootings, bombings, and related violence at Columbine High School in Jefferson County, Colorado, in April 1999 sent shock waves across the nation unlike any school violence incident in our past, including the various shootings in the prior 18 months. All of these incidents combined to create the most significant shift in the history of education in terms of thinking about the security and crisis preparedness components of school safety.

As one educator at one of my workshops stated, "We now define school safety from two very different perspectives: pre-Columbine and post-Columbine."

Post-Columbine Incidents

Educators across the nation experienced the impact of the Columbine incident both emotionally and practically on a day-to-day basis almost immediately after the incident. A number of bomb threats, actual homemade devices, death threats, and various other scares hit schools of all levels across the country. Many educators found themselves dealing with the effects of these incidents by trying to undo the decades of neglect in security and crisis preparedness almost overnight.

It is important to recognize that there were at least three levels of post-Columbine incidents taking place in schools across the nation. These included the following:

- A small number of plots and threats of violence planned prior to the Columbine incident that came to light shortly thereafter
- A significant volume of copycat or spin-off offenses, which came about as a result of, and also played upon the fears generated by, the Columbine incident (it is worth noting that even though they were often referred to as copycat offenses, this did not minimize the importance of having an appropriate response and serious concern by school officials)
- A noticeable number of cases in which teachers, administrators, and other school officials detected indicators of possible violence and threats before that actually occurred thanks to their heightened awareness created by the attention to the Columbine situation

This heightened awareness may very well have detected things that had gone unnoticed far before April 1999 but that now were suddenly more visible to those who were working with kids. This heightened awareness and action among school personnel has also led to increased communication between school and law enforcement authorities, including improved reporting of incidents to police, which in turn has generated continued media coverage and public attention to overall school safety and crisis issues.

In short, without a doubt, the close of the 1998-1999 school year was a blessing for most school and law enforcement officials, not to mention to the number of students themselves whose school lives were disrupted daily by threats of violence.

Media Mania

The media, as in any other high-profile incident of violence or national interest, worked diligently to ensure that every possible angle of the various school shootings, particularly the Columbine tragedy, was well covered in all forms, from print and television to radio and Internet news. Headlines ranged from "breaking news" coverage of the events and their follow-up developments as they unfolded, to weeks and months of "expert analysis." Ironically, the so-called expert analysis was frequently given by individuals who rarely (if ever) worked with kids, violent kids in schools, or in the elementary or secondary school security field.

The combination of media coverage, copycat or spin-off incidents, heightened awareness and action by educators, improved communication between schools and law enforcement, and stepped up enforcement and preparedness efforts created a cycle that kept school safety in the forefront from the times of the various incidents to the very time that this book is being published.

Parents Awaken

The series of shootings and, in particular, the Columbine incident, mobilized parents to call and visit schools, board meetings, and other public forums to find out if their children are actually safe in schools. Nothing I have observed in my 15 years of experience in education has brought more parents out on an ongoing basis than the Columbine tragedy. Unfortunately, this voicing of concerns illustrated not only the common reactive nature of Americans on security issues following a tragedy but also revealed that there has been a silent majority of parents who, although concerned about the safety of their child's school before these incidents, simply assumed that security and crisis preparedness issues were a priority of school officials.

Ironically, the silence of this silent majority was actually a major factor contributing to the neglect of proactive security and crisis measures by many school administrators. Because these administrators typically heard only from an isolated parent or the usual "squeaky wheel" parents who complained when administrators took visible steps to improve security and crisis preparedness, many assumed that the complainers represented the majority when, to the contrary, they did not. The administrators were therefore acting on their false perception that parents had no desire for action on school safety, thereby fueling their denial, image concerns, "politricks," and related inaction on these issues.

This picture quickly changed after April 1999. Parents—the majority having a legitimate reason to inquire—began knocking down doors and ringing the phones off the hook at most school offices. And now that the parents—that is, the taxpayers, voters, and sources of funding approval for many districts—were making demands, educators had to respond.

"Politricks": The Root of All Evil?

The Political Prostitution of School Safety

Parents were not the only ones to take notice of the importance of school safety. As parental and other public voices grew louder, politicians at all levels quickly saw the increased public attention on school safety and, as is the nature of a political beast, wasted no time to prostitute the issue—and themselves—for political gain. This came in various forms, including, but not limited to, the use of school violence incidents in the gun control debate, to promote pet legislative projects, as a campaign platform, to further political party ideology, as a topic to sponsor public forums or hearings, or sometimes simply as a focal point to create legislation just to show that they were responding to the public's concerns.

It is worth noting that there are a number of elected officials at the local, state, and national level who were interested in youth violence, school safety, and related issues far before the high-profile school incidents of 1997 to 1999. In Indiana, for example, state officials had been working for years on security and crisis preparedness issues. After this string of violent incidents, efforts there and in similar places simply focused on refining and building on an already proven track record. And, even in those places where attention to these issues was given only after the crisis incidents, there was some very productive dialogue, consideration, and action given to filling some gaps and more sincerely to meeting needs with action instead of rhetoric.

Although it took not one, but multiple tragedies, school safety, security, and crisis preparedness have finally reached the top of our public agenda.

The National Political Spin in General. In addition to the various uses—or misuses—of school safety for political purposes named above, the political play on school safety at the national level between 1997 and 1999 was exceptionally intriguing.

The use of the shootings incidents to further gun control politics was particularly evident. Although I choose not to get into taking a public political position on gun control itself, I would argue that the exploitation and manipulation of public attention on school safety in the gun control debate reinforces the belief that some politicians will stoop to any level to further a political cause. Although one gun in any school is unquestionably one too many, it is ironic that more legislators claiming concern about school safety have not been holding hearings and debates about the most common and growing types of weapons in schools: box cutters, knives, razor blades, and other bladed weapons.

On the positive side, some accurate testimony did get slipped into the records of various legislative hearings, including those of the U.S. Congress. On May 6, 1999, I testified before a Senate Committee hearing on school safety about issues including the historically unbalanced approach to school safety, the political nature of school safety at the local level, the inaccuracy of data nationally on school crime, the lack of research on security and crisis preparedness strategies, and the need for more resources to address the security and crisis preparedness components (*ESEA: School Safety*, 1999). In monitoring legislative hearings and activities across the nation for the two years prior to my testimony, I identified this particular hearing as the first one since the initial shooting incident in 1997 that actually included a career school security professional to provide testimony about school security needs nationwide. How ironic that those who deal full-time with school security and school policing issues are often the last ones consulted for advice on this very topic!

The Democrat and Republican Spin. One of the more interesting spin jobs on the national level is the ongoing sparring between the Democrats and Republicans on the school safety issue. Over the two-year period of high-profile school violence incidents, the political spin between the two has fallen along the following lines:

1. Following the school shootings of late 1997 and early 1998, the Clinton administration came under fire for not responding quickly enough to address what appeared to be an ongoing, growing problem of school shootings.

2. In response to the attack, the administration generated a number of high-profile initiatives, including production of several reports and statistical summaries on school safety issues, several high-level conferences on the topic, and a number of grant programs that included varying levels of focus on school safety.

3. Administration critics retaliated by suggesting that the administration's responses, along with the actual incidents themselves, verified that schools are unsafe and that such an acknowledgment supports the call for parental choice, vouchers, and related programs.

4. The administration, and in particular the U.S. Department of Education, backpedaled and has since incorporated the company line "Schools are the safest place in the community" into their public sound bites, adding, if necessary, "But one incident is one too many, so here is what we are doing to prevent future incidents."

The result of this political game playing is a clear fence-walking effort, especially by the Department of Education, to the point that astute observers can actually predict when the company line sound bite will come out of the mouth of department officials interviewed about school safety.

One of the more interesting examples of the spin was the August 1999 release of data by the U.S. Department of Education claiming a 31% reduction in expulsions for firearms nationwide in the 1997-1998 school year from the previous year. Although Department of Education officials acknowledged that the report was flawed, Secretary Riley still held a press conference to boast that fewer young people are carrying guns or taking them into schools; that is, he reiterated the company line that schools are the safest place in the community (U.S. Department of Education, 1999). Not long after the press conference, however, a closer look at data from several states revealed that the report included underreported data, as well as apples-to-oranges comparisons in which expulsions for all weapons in one year were compared to expulsions for firearms only in the second year, yet the Department of Education still claimed that there were dramatic reductions, which, in essence, was not always the case.

Although I believe that gun incidents in schools are likely to decline, due in part to increased enforcement and prevention efforts, I also see an increase in the use of bladed weapons, such as knives, box cutters, and razor blades. This, however, appears to be rarely discussed by Department of Education or other officials. It is also clear that although there are many positive school safety-related initiatives sponsored or funded by the U.S. Department of Education, there is also a political agenda driving some of the reports, figures, press conferences, and other messages coming from that department, and probably others, at the federal level. Unfortunately, the average parent and citizen holds no clue to this manipulation or the political nature of school safety, thereby inappropriately believing most, if not all, of what these sources report.

Spin From the Education Organizations. Elected politicians were not the only people focusing on the best possible spin to put on school safety issues. Many educators, and particularly some of their professional organizations, also wasted no time stressing that schools are the safest place in the community. Increasing parental inquiries and demands, combined with constant media coverage, added an excessive amount of pressure on educators at all levels to take action that many did not feel was appropriate and that some, but not all, had been working diligently to avoid taking for years.

As momentum continued strongly against educators, to the point where they could no longer hold the traditional position that school safety could adequately be addressed through discipline, prevention, and intervention programs alone, many scrambled behind the scenes for answers on how to manage the overpowering push to deal with the security and crisis preparedness for the here and now. Damage control efforts were evident in the actions of some professional education associations, as they jumped quickly to produce documents, conferences, and any other resource possible to support their members in dealing with what was turning out to be nothing short of hysteria in some communities. Even so, a number of these associations turned to nonspecialists, consultants, or school staff with minimal experience in school security to provide their training, articles, and other deliverables. This response begs the question as to whether anyone had really received the message that this area is a specialized and detailed professional discipline field, not just something anyone can do.

Although I agree that the post-Columbine overreaction across the nation was clearly overwhelming, it is also realistic to acknowledge that overall the education community was unquestionably being "bitten in the behind" for their years of neglect in dealing with the security and crisis preparedness components of school safety.

Misused and Abused Sound Bites. Department of Education officials and professional associations are certainly not the only ones to practice spin efforts. It is important, however, for the general public to recognize that the messages they have been receiving, especially at the national level, are loaded with hidden political agendas far beyond the scope of what is known by the average citizen and even some experienced professionals in the field. Some of the most commonly misused sound bites in the media include the following:

1. *The media has created the problem.* Certainly the media has played a role, but they cannot be blamed for the entire problem of youth and school violence any more than can educators alone, parents alone, or other single entities. To place the entire responsibility on the media, especially for the purpose of taking the focus off what schools and others should be doing to reduce the risks, is little more than finger-pointing.

2. *Schools are the safest place in the community.* First, there is no consistent method of collecting data nationwide on school crime, so school crime figures are based typically on limited research studies, which are often grossly overgeneralized, or on crimes reported to law enforcement or government agencies, which we know from experience are grossly underreported for a variety of political and administrative reasons (Trump, 1998). Nevertheless, this statement is generally quite accurate; the real question, however, is "Safer than what?" If 15 kids are killed in a school and 25 in that community, then, yes, the school is statistically safer. But what does that mean to the 15 kids killed in the school and to their families? And, when considering the more common scenario of a child being bullied, assaulted, and extorted in school each day, does this child and his or her parents really care what the administrator's statistics show when they are the constant victims of school violence?

3. *It is community violence, not school violence.* Again, standing alone, this is a true statement. The fact that schools reflect the violence in the larger society, however, simply does not negate the school's responsibility to take some risk reduction measures to prevent such occurrences from happening. If a local shopping mall is the site of ATM holdups, rapes, carjackings, and other crimes, the mall most likely did not create the violence. Patrons, however, would certainly expect it to improve security and take some risk reduction measures to prevent future incidents from occurring, even though the violence is a reflection of the broader community and not the mall's creation per se. Why should we expect anything less from our schools?

The issue is not that society should believe that Columbine-like incidents are happening daily at every American school. On the whole, most schools are generally safe, and most educators want students and staff to be in a secure and welcoming environment. We cannot, however, fall prey to the continued denial and "politricks" that have characterized the past several decades in terms of how we address—or, more appropriately, have not addressed—school security and crisis preparedness issues.

Paranoia Prevails

The constant barrage of messages about school safety contributed to states of near paranoia in many schools and communities in the months immediately after the Columbine tragedy. In spite of the best efforts of politicians and "educrats" to control the runaway media and hysteria, the majority of them were unable to regain quick control, as they have been so used to doing over the years in responding to this issue. Educators were now backed into a corner and had to turn to Plan B.

PR Campaigns and Levy Leverage

In response to public pressure and its accompanying paranoia, many school officials across the nation spent the last part of the 1998-1999 school year, and an unprecedented amount of time during the summer before the opening of the 1999-2000 school year, addressing school safety. Unfortunately, far too many spent their time on doing something for the sake of doing something rather than on truly doing something and doing it properly. In fact, one superintendent called me to request school security consulting services and, when asked exactly what he needed, replied, "I really don't care what you come here and do, just as long as I can issue a press release to say that I had you here."

The drive to act resulted in a number of school districts focusing on physical and tangible forms of security. Additional manpower, security equipment, ID cards, see-through bookbags, locked doors, and related measures were often implemented, in large part because they are visible, physical, and tangible actions that school administrators could point to in showing their students, staff, parents, and the media that they were indeed "doing something" related to school security. Although these measures alone are often necessary and appropriate in a number of schools, many were implemented post-Columbine for public relations purposes rather than to address a specific security threat.

The result of such initiatives is the creation of a false sense of security, especially if strategies are not properly implemented and consistently enforced. Professional school security programs rest on a foundation of consistently enforced security policies and procedures, ongoing training for all staff on security threat trends and strategies, implementing recommendations from professional assessments of a school or district's security needs, and the creating and testing crisis preparedness guidelines for handling serious incidents. Unfortunately, these foundation measures are much harder to show to members of the school community in the short term, but they stand to be much more promising in improving school security in the long run.

It is also not surprising that little time lapsed before many school officials, already notorious for spinning the worst situations into a light more favorable for their image interests, began manipulating public fear about school safety into something beneficial to their
districts. A number of school leaders in the fall of 1999 began by organizing be-
hind-the-scenes efforts to identify security needs, and in particular those with financial
costs, such as physical improvements and equipment, to use them as leverage for gaining
community support for the passage of planned tax levies. Although the majority doing so
were also genuinely concerned about safety, it is unfortunate that they did not miss a beat
in taking a series of tragedies and spinning them politically for school district gain.

A Call for Common Sense

A number of absurd proposals and theories developed in the aftermath of the various
school shootings. Arguments from an academic perspective included one that suggested
the presence of police and security measures actually created violence by communicating
to the children that they were in an environment of fear and distrust. Such an argument
holds about as much water as the proposition that the person supporting such a ludicrous
argument should leave his or her home windows and doors open while they are work so
that they do not communicate fear and distrust to potential burglars!

An equally absurd idea floating around at the time centered on the suggestion that
legislation should be passed to allow school staff to be armed with weapons. The support-
ers of this legislation obviously never worked in schools, or else they would know that, if
such legislation did pass and school staff were armed, roughly 50% would lose their guns
by the end of the first period class, another 25% would accidentally shoot themselves during second period, and the remaining 25% would have their guns stolen from them by the
end of third period! Although this analysis is only meant to add a bit of humor to the absurd, we are likely to see such strange proposals resurface if further high-profile incidents
occur.

Fortunately, most educators did the right things after Columbine by seeking out a balanced approach for addressing school security and crisis preparedness. A number of veteran administrators worked with their staff, students, parents, emergency service providers, and others in the school community to evaluate and refine policies and to enhance
staff training and awareness on managing and preventing crisis situations. Likewise, an
increasing number turned to outside specialists, including law enforcement agencies and
experienced school security consultants, to conduct security assessments and develop
their crisis preparedness guidelines.

The most common question asked by school administrators has been "How can I improve school security without creating a prisonlike environment?" Ironically, the best answer to this question came from a group of students at the high school in Bruni, Texas, on a
day when I worked with staff and students over the summer following the Columbine incident. When asked how they would improve school safety if they were the superintendent, they responded with three primary suggestions:

1. *Deal with the issue of disrespect.* They indicated that student-to-student disrespect, as
well as student-to-staff disrespect, was one of the top issues that schools need to address.
In short, they were talking about improving the school climate.

2. *Enforce the rules that are already on the books.* Students stressed that oftentimes adults, both teachers and administrators, do not consistently enforce the rules that are already in the discipline handbooks. Their point was that we do not need new rules, but we do need to ensure that the rules we have are enforced in a firm, fair, and consistent manner.

3. *Improve security, but don't create a prison.* The students indicated that they had no problem with strategies for improving school security, such as school resource officers, for example, as long as the officers could relate to the kids and still be firm in enforcing the rules. They did, however, note that they did not feel that an officer was needed at every door: Schools should tighten up security but not go to extremes.

In looking back on the debates, expert analysis, and other adult discussions following the school violence incidents between 1997 and 1999, the suggestions from the students were the most rational and enlightening ones I heard. They reinforce the message, which I repeat here, that we need to take a balanced and rational approach to school safety. Most important is that adults, unlike kids, often overlook the practical solutions and commonsense perspectives needed to make a real difference in improving school safety.

2

Lessons Learned
From School Crisis Incidents

If we can learn nothing but two things from the experiences of the victims of school crises, remember that "it can happen here" and that there are things that can be done to prevent and prepare for such tragedies.

Most educators would describe themselves as lifelong learners in addition to being teachers of others. Sadly enough, it took multiple tragedies over a period of roughly 18 months before many educators, and many Americans in general, learned that school shootings, bombings, and other violent incidents like those witnessed from 1997 to 1999 could, indeed, happen in any community in the nation. Even after the incidents, I crossed paths with a number of school officials (ironically in security and crisis preparedness workshops) who still flatly said that they do not believe that a school crisis *could* occur in their community.

It is important for school officials to practice what is preached in the education community: Learn from the experiences of others. School officials cannot do the job alone, however; emergency service providers, parents, students, and community leaders must also examine how, or perhaps even if, they will be mentally and operationally prepared for a crisis.

School and community leaders can begin their preparations by learning from the experiences of those who have already experienced such tragedies.

Be Prepared, Not Scared

The two most common messages heard over and over in news and other accounts of school crisis incidents have been

- "We never thought it could happen here," and
- "There was nothing we could do to train or prepare for such a tragedy."

If nothing else is remembered from the actual school crises that have occurred in our nation, school and community officials must learn from the experiences of others that it *can* happen here, regardless of where *here* is located, and that although every incident cannot be prevented, there are steps
that can be taken to reduce the risks for such incidents, and preparations that
can be made to more effectively manage a crisis, should one occur.

It is human nature for individuals to deny, or at least to avoid thinking
about, a possible tragedy in their school or community. And educators
should not go to work each day in fear or in a state of paranoia. However,
one of the best ways to increase the risk of experiencing a crisis or of being
victimized by violence is to let down one's guard and to operate with a
mind-set isolated from reality.

Educators should not be scared; they must, however, be prepared.

Priority One: Crisis Preparedness

A debriefing of officials from several cities that experienced school
shootings in 1997 and 1998 identified as one of the primary lessons from
their experiences the importance of having a well-defined crisis response
team, one with the ability to communicate and effectively collaborate on responding to and managing crisis incidents (Reisman, 1998). Because a school
crisis quickly becomes a community crisis, it is important for response teams
to include coordination not only among the key players within the school
district, but also with those in the broader community. Crisis preparedness is
also an ongoing process, not a solitary event, and so it requires testing and
exercising crisis guidelines, not simply putting together a fancy document
and leaving it in the principal's office until a crisis strikes the school.

Cathy Danyluk, Safe School Consultant for the Indiana Department of
Education, best described the importance of preparedness when she noted,
"The offenders in school shooting incidents came to school with a plan. So
should educators" (personal communication, May 3, 1998). The only difference, she added, is that "educators need to make sure that they have tested
and exercised their plans more thoroughly than those who actually have
thought out their own plan to commit the offenses."

Prevention: An Equal Priority

The first line of effective prevention planning is having comprehensive,
effective school security and crisis preparedness measures in place. Unfortunately, these items are often not viewed as prevention. However, most school
security personnel and school resource officers report that they have prevented a greater number of potentially violent situations than they have re-
acted to incidents culminating in an arrest.

Other specific prevention and intervention issues and strategies will be
discussed further in Chapter 4, along with the issues of so-called profiling
and the supposed early warning signs of violent offenders.

Deal With Small Problems

Most veteran school administrators and security personnel tend to agree that dealing with small problems while they are still small will prevent larger problems from arising down the road. The three most common "small problems" that trigger more serious school violence incidents are

1. "He said/she said/they said" rumors

2. Boyfriend or girlfriend conflicts or rumors

3. Disrespect, or "dissin' " in the words of the kids, both real and perceived (Trump, 1998)

Although educators realistically cannot spend all day dealing with each of these types of conflicts, they should exercise care not to overlook or dismiss these problems without addressing them in an appropriate and meaningful manner.

Those who fail to deal with these issues should not be surprised at the result of their inaction. The student who accidentally bumps into someone in the hallway at 7:30 a.m. and exchanges derogatory remarks instead of offering a simple "excuse me" may very well be the same person who pulls out a razor blade and slashes the other person in the face after school. Disrespect, along with the rumor mill of "he said/she said" comments, can quickly transform a small conflict into a major incident in very little time.

The issue of disrespect, in particular, warrants much closer attention by adults than it is often given. Disrespect may be real or perceived, and it may come in a variety of forms, including the following:

- Staring, "dirty looks" or "doggin' " (as it sometimes known today), eye rolling, lip smacking, or other nonverbal communications intended to mock, disrespect, or intimidate another student

- Verbal put-downs

- Rumors and gossip

- Bullying and teasing

- Pushing, shoving, hallway horseplay, or similar physical intimidation, often dismissed by adults as being too minor for their involvement

- Alienation and isolation (i.e., making someone an outcast)

These are a few examples, but certainly not an exhaustive list.

So many incidents of in-school violence, even some of the higher-profile cases and cases involving gang conflicts, often start with these lower-profile forms of disrespect and aggressive behavior. Goldstein (1999) best describes this, arguing that

we as a society have far too often ignored the very manifestations of low-level aggression that, when rewarded, grow (often rapidly) into those several forms of often intractable high-level aggression that are currently receiving a great deal of society's attention. (p. 2)

The small problems described above, and the resulting high-profile problems that result if they go unattended, represent a perfect example of how this applies to school settings.

School Climate

The need to deal with disrespect and other lower-level forms of aggression illustrates the importance of addressing school climate issues in general. Although the tendency of educators to focus solely on these issues and not on security and crisis preparedness has created a critical imbalance in the approach to school safety, a focus on school climate should not be dismissed or minimized in an attempt to catch up on security and crisis preparedness deficiencies. Respect, sensitivity to diversity, appropriate language and behavior, peaceable conflict resolution, and related characteristics of a positive and supportive learning environment play significant roles in reducing safety risks.

Efforts to improve school climate by dealing with these issues must be ongoing and reinforced on a regular basis. A number of schools with warm, welcoming, and trusting environments, as well as balanced security measures and comprehensive crisis preparedness guidelines, have actually developed themes around climate issues that are reinforced through various education and communications strategies on a daily basis. Posters, signs, activities, and other measures centered on these themes, although somewhat similar to media advertisements in terms of their stand-out techniques and repetition, do stick with children and staff, in many cases becoming ingrained in their thoughts and actions.

Overcoming Student Denial

Denial of school safety concerns and issues has increasingly become an issue over the past decade, and has especially surfaced following recent school violence tragedies. However, the focus has primarily been on denial by school officials, parents, politicians, and other adults in the broader school community, when, in fact, there is also a level of denial present in many students. In a number of discussions with youths, I have discovered that the "It can't happen here" mentality is as equally present with students as it is with adults.

It is possible, if not probable, that one reason for student denial of the potential for a high-profile school violence incident is that they believe and are modeling the denial of the many adults with whom they come into contact. It is also reasonable to conclude, however, that youths, and in particular teens, often have a false sense of security generated by their perception that they know other students in the school and that none of these other students would commit a shooting or other major offense. Combined with their natural perception of self-invincibility, the confidence gained from the belief that they know each other and that, from their perspectives, these other youths would not commit such offenses, actually fosters a tendency not to see the potential for a critical incident to occur.

Overcoming youth denial is as sensitive an issue as overcoming adult denial. A number of educators believe that by discussing these incidents head-on, they will actually create a fear in students that otherwise would not exist. Unfortunately, such an adult mind-set only fosters both more denial and an unrealistic mind-set in students, who often seem to handle crises better than some adults do anyway.

The real focus needs to be placed not on *if* the adults will discuss school safety issues and concerns with students, but on *how* they will do so. Discussions of this type need to be honest, and need to offer direct explanations of safety concerns, the rationale behind such school safety strategies as lockdowns, and the importance of the procedures and practices put in place to deal with security and crisis situations. Students typically understand and appreciate such communications, and will respond as desired in a drill or an actual crisis.

A Switch From "Snitch"

The need for educators to create ways for students, parents, and other individuals to report threats, rumored violence, and other safety concerns is another important lesson learned from recent school crises. Students and others often know about a potential violent act before the incident occurs, yet many times this information does not make its way to those who can prevent the violence until after an incident has happened. Reasons for the withholding of information range from fear of reprisals if the reporting person is identified, to denial of the "We never thought that he would actually do what he said he was going to do" or "Kids will be kids" sort.

The most common way adults find out about a student bringing a weapon to school is by other students reporting it. Kids basically want to know that two things will occur when they do report: First, that they will remain anonymous, and, second, that someone will follow up on what they report.

School staff members need to realize that this anonymity means not only that they will not tell other students, but also that they will not tell other staff members aside from an administrator or other official authorized to act on the information.

Students also need to know about the follow-up when they report something. For example, one teacher shared her concern about a student who had not attended school since the day that the student reported seeing a gun fall from another student's backpack. The principal had promised that he would meet her in the same stairwell the day following the incident so that the student could identify this otherwise unknown gun-toting student, but the principal did not show up. The student then decided to not attend school again, because she perceived that her report was not taken seriously and that there was not going to be a follow-up as promised.

In addition to assuring anonymity and doing proper follow-up on reports, we also need to reeducate children that providing information related to threats to safety is not "snitching," but instead may indeed be life-saving. The life saved may be that of the reporting person, his or her friend, or others in the school. This education process needs to take place quickly and thoroughly in all schools, beginning at the elementary level.

A variety of mechanisms have been created to promote an anonymous and more timely reporting of concerns about violence, including the following:

- Telephone hotlines, within schools or school districts, consisting of a dedicated phone line with an answering machine that is checked regularly
- Government hotlines through city, county, or state police, education, and other agencies
- Commercial hotline services that offer to operate a fee-based 24-hour, 7-day per week staffed hotline for school districts
- Hotlines connected to the school system's voice mail service, which activates an administrator's pager once a message is left to alert the administrator of a new call
- Electronic mail hotlines, where students can send e-mail tips to designated officials, thereby capitalizing on the interest children have in the technological world

Regardless of how it is done, the mechanism for reporting must be made very widely known to students and must be promoted on an ongoing basis in order to get the most use of it.

Communicate About Safety

Just as tip lines need to be promoted and reinforced regularly, so does the issue of school safety itself. Educators often falsely assume that students, staff, parents, and others know that safety is a top concern for administrators. School officials must recognize that they have multiple audiences—students, staff, parents, community, and media—and that they must regularly communicate to these audiences that safety is indeed a priority at their school.

How can they communicate this message? Some simple ways include the following:

1. *Practicing what is preached!* The daily actions of administrators and staff provide the strongest messages to students. They must see that the adults are not only "talking the talk," but also are "walking the walk."

2. *Making public address announcements and assemblies.* Educators remind students about school rules from time to time throughout the school year, yet

they often do not talk specifically about safety. A periodic reminder of its importance can certainly do no harm.

3. *Encouraging posters, banners, and other student-led activities.* Get students involved in identifying safety concerns and strategies for improving school climate and safety. Help them to spread their message through signs, banners, and other promotional contests.

4. *Faculty meetings.* Although faculty meeting time is often limited and the agenda is typically full, it only takes a few seconds to remind staff periodically of the importance of things such as locking doors, greeting and reporting strangers, and other safety issues.

5. *Parent newsletters.* PTA newsletters and other parent communications provide a great opportunity to remind parents and guardians of school safety initiatives, safety-related rules and procedures, and the need for parents to talk with their children about safety issues.

6. *Education programs.* Student assemblies, staff professional day programs, parent workshops, and other educational opportunities should be provided on safety-related topics.

7. *Collaborative efforts.* Work with law enforcement, fire, medical, and other emergency service officials to develop and test security and crisis plans. This not only helps the school formulate effective guidelines, but also communicates to public safety officials that school leaders are serious about school safety.

8. *Media messages.* Be accessible to the media, and do not be afraid to address safety issues head-on when asked by a reporter. Learn how to work with the media, not how to try to get away from them.

School safety and crisis preparedness planning are processes, not events. Regular communication and awareness of safety-related issues will help keep these issues in the forefront while allowing educators to prevent paranoia and fear by sending balanced, rational messages during noncrisis times.

Listen to Kids and Parents

One group of students had some very serious complaints about the installation of metal detectors in their school. Although most adults expected these complaints to focus on the delays in getting into school because of the inspections, student complaints actually centered on their belief that the adults were not checking their backpacks thoroughly enough when they activated the metal detector! At another school, one student, who was the victim of an extortion but saw no action taken when he reported it to an administrator, asked, "How can we learn to be serious about crime when we don't see crime being dealt with seriously in our own school?"

The awakening of the silent majority of parents to school safety issues following the high-profile national incidents of violence provided a clear indicator to school officials that safety is, indeed, a top priority to parents. Although no administrator wants to experience what occurred during and after the Columbine tragedy in mid-1999, educators should keep in the back of their minds the extent of parental uproar about school safety that occurred after these incidents. In fact, progressive administrators will remember to seek out input and recommendations periodically from both students and parents, in addition to staff and outside public safety officials, at times during the school year when there is not a crisis incident triggering them to do so.

Although facts and data should largely drive decisions, educators and safety officials must also address perceptions about school safety. Actual school conditions may be significantly safer than they are perceived to be by some members of the school community, but these perceptions must be acknowledged and addressed. Perception can often turn into reality when left unchecked, and school administrators should ensure that they communicate about school safety accurately, clearly, and regularly.

Rely on Local Data

National data on school crime and violence are extremely flawed and misleading for a variety of reasons, as discussed in Chapter 1, so it is not uncommon to see two reports from the same national source identify conflicting trends within weeks of their publication. In light of the political and logistical constraints prohibiting accurate national school violence data, school officials would be wise to focus on local data to help identify security threat trends and areas for preventive action. Such local data would include school discipline data, school crime data, police crime data for the communities in which students reside, staff surveys, parent surveys, student surveys, and focus groups.

The value of student surveys and input should not be underestimated. Students often see things differently and much more clearly than their adult counterparts. Adult perspectives tend to be clouded with personal biases, political agendas, philosophical twists, and, in general, more theoretical and conceptual thinking than those of students.

For example, in one discussion with adults and students about who or what is responsible for school violence, the majority of adults tended to blame guns and the media, whereas kids identified the individual offenders and their actions as the source primarily responsible for the violence. The students were much more practical and realistic, whereas adults tended to point fingers, place blame, and spout rhetoric. It was not surprising, then, that the kids also had more practical and realistic strategies for preventing and managing school violence, too.

Neglect of the Privileged?

In one crisis preparedness workshop, a principal asked why the school violence incidents of the late 1990s seemed to be happening only in rural or suburban areas. "Is it just the revenge of the nerds?" he asked seriously, suggesting that the shooters may have been "getting even" for years of harassment and being made outcasts from the more popular students.

Although it is very likely that harassment and disrespect toward the offenders may have played a significant role in their violent outbursts, it is unlikely that these factors were the sole causes of these incidents. Other likely factors include the following:

1. *Suburban and rural communities have generally looked at violence and crisis issues as inner-city problems.* The level of security and crisis preparedness in these cities has therefore been minimal or, more often than not, nonexistent. Unfortunately, the "We never thought it would happen here" mentality was, and in some places still is, alive and well. Security and crisis preparedness measures have therefore, at least until the high profile school shootings, been seen as unnecessary and alarmist in the eyes of many suburban and rural educators, parents, and public officials because, in their minds, "those things" only happen in the inner city.

2. *Race, money, and politics are directly related to the perception that violence is an inner-city issue.* While working in a predominantly minority inner-city school district, for example, I observed that the common adult was focused on arresting and prosecuting students caught with drugs in schools—period. This was certainly a legal and appropriate response. In contrast, when I worked in a suburban school district, the message was to get treatment for the children caught with drugs, but to think twice as to whether school officials should really be so punitive as to pursue arrest and prosecution. In essence, many suburban and rural areas, especially those where residents are predominantly white and affluent or are relatives of politically connected or highly positioned professionals, have sheltered their children from the legal consequences for their criminal acts and, in many cases, have even sheltered them from disciplinary consequences by school administrators for violations of school rules.

3. *Parents and children often focus too much on material items.* "I bought everything for this kid, and he still turned out to be violent," one mother said at a parent workshop on school safety. "I could not even go into his bedroom because he told me that it is against state law," she added. Although urban parents may also overindulge their children with material items, it is especially predominant in many suburban and rural communities, where parents often have more resources to buy things for their children and to give them money whenever they request it. This focus on material wealth, when coupled with a lack of discipline, teaches too many children that they have to work for very little, and that money, not time and love, are the most important things parents have to give them. Add together money, mobility, and few, if any, consequences for misbehaviors, and you have a formula for disaster. (And, no, there was no such state law prohibiting parents from going into their child's bedroom in their own home.)

4. *Denial and neglect are factors, too.* Many children from more affluent families have easier access to professional assistance such as counseling,

drug treatment, and other mental health services, but this certainly does not mean that they get the services. In fact, because of concerns about family image, parental guilt, and just plain denial, many suburban and rural children do not receive the mental health and professional services that they truly need. Such circumstances foster trouble, and children become like a number of pots just waiting to boil over. Violent outbursts by children from suburban and rural areas should therefore really be no more of a surprise than the outbursts by children from inner-city communities.

5. *Inner-city schools are typically far ahead in the game when it comes to preventing violence.* Although many large urban school districts may have a larger volume of violent incidents than their suburban and rural counterparts, the reality is that many of these inner-city schools have addressed security procedures, crisis planning, and similar risk reduction and awareness measures far sooner than these other districts. More doors are routinely secured, visitors and strangers are challenged more quickly, teachers and staff are better trained and experienced in dealing with crime and violence issues, crisis preparedness plans have long been established and tested in real life as well as in training, early warning signs are detected by staff more quickly, and so on. Meanwhile, in many suburban and rural schools, 40 out of 40 doors in one school could be found open at any given time until the recent spate of high-profile school violence incidents forced such schools to take precautions. Why should we be surprised that a violent incident could occur in suburban and rural schools, especially after considering that there has been little done in terms of security and crisis training, planning, and procedure implementation? If anything, we should be surprised that it has not happened sooner and more often!

There are a number of other potential factors that may very well play into the urban/suburban debate on school violence. Although the point is not to identify them all here, it is important that we stop acting so shocked and surprised when we hear of violence in our suburban and rural areas. In the words of veteran educator and internationally known presenter Steve Sroka, "The major difference between the inner city and suburban communities is that, in the suburbs, drugs and violence hide behind lawns, lawyers, and fences" (personal communication, September 4, 1999).

Train Emergency Services

One assistant principal commented at a recent school crisis conference that he had little confidence in the training and preparedness level of his community. When asked if he was referring to his school colleagues, he responded by saying, "No. I'm more confident that some of my teachers could diffuse a gunman than I am that our emergency service officials could do so." He went on to explain not only that the police department was extremely small with high personnel turnover, but also that the fire department was a volunteer department, and that the two departments had received little, if any, training in working with schools in a crisis.

This administrator's point is well taken, and, with no disrespect to the many dedicated emergency service providers in our country, it is more accurate than many people would like to imagine in a number of communities. Police and emergency service budgets not only typically represent one of the largest expenditure areas in any government budget, but they also tend to have relatively few funds available for training beyond that which is mandatory, particularly considering the volume and variety of violent, life-threatening situations faced by emergency service providers. Furthermore, manpower and other logistical constraints often limit the amount of cross training that can take place among the various types of emergency service agencies, such as police, fire, and medical units.

The need for a new training focus for safety personnel also came about as a result of the recent school shooting incidents. In particular, police SWAT teams, typically trained to set up a perimeter and secure the area until the conflict is de-escalated and resolved, must shift their focus on how to deal with active shooter situations. Instead of containing and de-escalating, officers are now training on how to search facilities and rescue building occupants from situations where perpetrators are actively shooting or otherwise violently attacking those inside.

In addition to the fact that many police, fire, and medical units do not train in working together, the majority of these entities across the nation have had, at best, limited exposure to the schools in their communities. Aside from responding to individual and isolated calls for specific incidents several times a year, many emergency service providers have been inside the schools only if their own children happen to attend. Add to this the historical denial and political approaches schools have taken in dealing with the police in particular, and it becomes clear that the majority of our emergency service providers have had extremely limited professional exposure to school facilities and personnel.

There have been improvements in school and law enforcement partnerships in the past 10 to 15 years, before the series of school shootings in the late 1990s, but these have typically focused more on classroom instruction, special event security, and information sharing. One exception is the school resource officer (SRO) concept, which has grown in popularity and effectiveness during this time period, and appropriately so. Still, from enforcement and tactical perspectives, the average police department typically has not specifically trained or prepared to prevent and manage a school-related crisis.

Media Lessons Learned

Schools, public safety agencies, and other community members are not the only ones to learn lessons from school violence tragedies. The media has increasingly come under fire for their coverage of school violence, and closer examinations of their coverage have drawn out some important lessons for them, too. For example, in its examination of the coverage of the school

shooting in Jonesboro, Arkansas, in 1998, The Freedom Forum (1998) issued
these recommendations for the media on covering school tragedies:

- Editors and news directors should establish guidelines and expectations, set standards for the behavior of journalists, avoid demonizing
  or glorifying suspects or victims, substantiate information, and know
  when to get the story off of the front page.

- Reporters and photographers should focus on the impact of the event
  on the entire community, avoid hyping an already big story, avoid
  jumping to conclusions and misrepresentation, and report on what
  worked properly and what went well in the response to the incident.

- All media representatives should work on a foundation of trust. They
  should also consider creating media pools to avoid creating a "media
  mob" situation.

Having provided, as a national school security consultant, over 300 interviews in the first three weeks following the Columbine crisis, I developed
a unique understanding of just how little most producers, editors, news directors, reporters, and other media representatives know about schools and,
in particular, about school security and crisis preparedness issues. This is not
an attack on the media. In fact, I am a strong advocate for opening the doors
and working with the media; however, it is time that the media look at their
own knowledge base and biases. I have often found reporters to be excellent
at conceptualizing, philosophizing, and theorizing about violence and society in general; however, when it comes time to zero in on specific short-term
actions that schools can take to reduce risks for school violence, the reporters
too often shift back to abstractions or generalizations.

Reporters love to talk about social ills, psychological issues, family dysfunction, and similar topics. Yet when it comes to talking about the importance of such basic security measures as reducing the numbers of open
doors, the importance and mechanics of a lockdown safety drill, or how politics interfere with improving school security, many reporters have tended to
brush these issues aside and revert to abstract, general, or broad concepts.
Although long-term behavior changes, societal institutions such as the family, and other overarching issues deserve attention and discussion, reporters
also need to focus on the little steps toward change and the obstacles in getting things done on a day-to-day basis; these, too, warrant as much attention
as the sometimes Utopian world people in our society believe exists and, in
turn, tend to like to discuss.

Reporters are also often too liberal in labeling interviewees as *school
safety experts* or gifting them with similar titles in the media blitz following a
school crisis when, in many cases, the individuals being interviewed have
little to no experience in working with school violence or with K-12 school
security issues. These individuals thereby become instant "experts" and, in
some cases, create a name for themselves in the field when, in reality, their
experience and knowledge base in these areas is quite limited. The end result

is that the public, along with legislators and others who are watching or read-ing, wrongly look at the "analysis" from these individuals as being accurate and worthy of action.

Fortunately, in my experience I have seen that the majority of reporters are good professionals who want to do quality work, and typically do so in spite of the fact that they work in a money-driven business full of pressures to produce stories in very short periods of time. A significant number of re-porters have dedicated time—oftentimes their own unpaid time—to learn more about the complexities of school safety and to go beyond the stereo-types of what school security and crisis preparedness is perceived to be to learn what it is in reality. Professional associations, such as the Education Writers Association, have also helped to further reporters' understanding of school violence by providing conferences and resources on the topic from a variety of professional perspectives.

It's What You Don't Know . . .

Everyone remembers the motherly advice, "It's what you don't know that might hurt you." Truer words were never spoken when it comes to school security and crisis preparedness. Although high-profile incidents cer-tainly provide a focus for learning important lessons, educators and others in the school community need to think about school security when there is *not* a crisis.

A number of reporters asked me after the Columbine incident whether or not it was a wake-up call for schools to do a better job at school security. My answer was simply that the question was not whether Columbine was a wake-up call, but whether or not as a society we would keep hitting the snooze button and going back to sleep. Educators need to concentrate on se-curity and crisis preparedness at all times, not just after a particular incident.

In fairness to educators, the tendency to react rather than act is a national trait. Americans focus on embassy security after an embassy bombing, workplace violence after an office shooting, and airline crashes after an air-line accident. Yet when these items are no longer in the headlines, Americans put the issues on the back burners and move on to other "hot" topics, to re-turn to these types of issues only when the next crisis arises. Oddly enough, we then spend even more time wondering aloud why such incidents con-tinue to happen!

This tendency to run hot and cold is even more entrenched in the educa-tion community because of the absence of any type of accurate, strong, coor-dinated, and ongoing national information source on school crimes, vio-lence, and related prevention, intervention, enforcement, and crisis preparedness strategies. There is a growing number of well-funded think tanks, centers, and institutes that study, collect, and analyze information on school and youth violence; however, many of these efforts are politically driven or politically funded, and tend to be limited in scope and usefulness to educators on the front lines for a variety of reasons. Although there are dozens of theories on the causes of school violence and hundreds, if not thousands, of different violence prevention programs claiming to be the answer to school and youth violence, the reality is that we do not know even how many crimes are committed in schools each year because our data collection mechanisms are inadequate and school-based crimes are underreported on a national level.

As a part of our company's business services, I follow national news stories about school safety through a variety of traditional and new technology sources, in addition to working in the field with those on the front lines. The average educator and administrator in our workshops turns out to be shocked when we show him or her the cases of stabbing, hostage taking, bombing, bomb threats, and other violent episodes taking place across the nation on an ongoing basis that do not make their local news. Although I do not believe that school violence should dominate the headlines each day, I do believe that educators need to recognize that, in terms of security and crisis preparedness, they should pay attention not just to the higher-profile incidents, but also to what they do *not* hear about or see each day, because these incidents best give us an understanding of the patterns, trends, and issues with which we need to be concerned.

Overnight Experts, Gurus, and Gadgets

One of the foremost lessons learned from the school violence tragedies has been that educators must be prepared for the attack of the overnight experts, charlatans, and product-pushers who emerge after a crisis or crises to exploit these incidents and the resulting state of fear for personal or business gain. Following the series of school violence incidents in the late 1990s, everyone from academicians to politicians—and even former magicians!—began spouting their theories and "solutions" for improving school safety. Likewise, an extraordinary number of security equipment and other vendors began popping out of the woodwork in an effort to get their products into the school marketplace, regardless of whether it was designed or tailored to fit there.

Overnight Experts and Charlatans Abound

In the months following the first series of school shootings, and particularly in those months following the tragedy at Columbine High School in April of 1999, my office was flooded with calls, letters, faxes, and e-mail messages from individuals looking to change careers, enter the consulting field, or sell products and services to educators to "prevent" such violent incidents from occurring in their schools. Here is a sample of some of the contacts we received, along with those we reviewed from various other sources:

- A former federal law enforcement agent wanted to buy all of my slides and videos so that he would go out to schools the following month to sell "his" services as a school security expert.

- Two military security specialists, one whose expertise included "special weapons site security" and the other whose expertise included being a "qualified expert with pistol, shotgun, and rifle," submitted unsolicited resumes because they wanted to be hired as school security expert consultants.

- Numerous educators and former educators, including a retired school personnel director and former principal, a current elementary school principal, a high school athletic coach, a former superintendent of a private school, and several educators advertising themselves as former law enforcement officers (although they had been law enforcement officers for only a few years and then spent several dozen years in education), were promoting themselves as school safety "experts."

- A number of potential investors sought to contribute funds to our company, even though we are a private firm and do not offer stock.

- Several academicians and researchers who, although their backgrounds had never included issues related to school security, now wanted to collaborate to seek funds for studying school violence prevention, security measures, and related issues.

- Dozens of current and former local and state law enforcement officers who had never worked in schools or with kids as a primary part of their law enforcement jobs, decided that their "expertise" in school safety offered more options for better income than did performing security functions off-duty at football games, basketball games, dances, or other security guard–type part-time jobs, and began consulting as school security specialists almost overnight. One contacted our office five times, pleading for me to "teach" him how to enter the school security consulting business because, as he said, "There is enough work out there for all of us to make a buck."

- School security "experts" whose backgrounds prior to the time of the shootings included being bodyguards, private detectives, drug counselors, security guard providers, insurance adjusters, magicians, and numerous other unrelated professions contacted us.

- Computer programmers offered new software designed to analyze student writing assignments to identify violent kids, develop threat assessment profiles by answering a series of questions, conduct risk assessments of schools, track school crime, and develop school crisis plans.

- A corporate conference planner sought to shift to a new career putting on school safety programs across the nation.

- A former federal law enforcement agent whose expertise prior to retirement included scientific laboratory operations, white collar crimes, and international drug cartels sent us an unsolicited resume. He wanted to discuss "how [his] experience would be of benefit" to our company in providing school security services.

- A group of former law enforcement officials, in addition to providing investigative services, threat assessments, and workplace violence prevention training, now offered school violence training to decrease serious behavioral incidents and increase student attendance and success rates.

- Dozens of security product vendors offered everything from ID cards to locks, fiber optics, surveillance cameras, digital imaging, web-based information services, and safety newsletters and publications, and every other product one could possibly imagine.

- Security consultants with backgrounds in providing services or consultation to utility companies, government agencies, embassies, private corporations, and other institutions unrelated to K-12 schools, became *school* security consultants almost overnight.

And the list goes on.

Although there are a number of experienced, educated, and qualified school security consultants across the nation, it is clear that there is also a significant number of individuals and companies who attempted to capitalize, in one way or another, on the tragedies and losses experienced at numerous schools across our nation. The majority of these individuals have little or no history of ongoing education in or experience with the field of school safety. Nevertheless, a number of schools hired such individuals or purchased such products, failing to realize that the costs of hiring a poorly selected, unqualified consultant, or of purchasing products for the sake of "doing something," will likely increase the very risks and liability that they were hoping to reduce.

Lessons Learned About "Experts"

A number of important lessons can be learned from these and other examples of overnight experts:

1. *Law enforcement or security experience alone does not automatically equate to school security expertise.* An individual may have an outstanding career in law enforcement, but this does not immediately make him or her a school security expert. There are unique differences between the law enforcement and security communities, and there are also unique differences between security in K-12 schools and security in other environments, such as military security, utility companies, or private industry. It is difficult to understand why some educators will accept individuals with no experience in working with children, schools, or K-12 school security as school security experts! School officials should not allow impressive titles and careers in other fields alone to command respect as a school security specialist.

2. *School administrators must learn to check for borderline backgrounds and misleading qualifications.* They need to examine the backgrounds of so-called school security experts to see whether they actually have experience in school-specific environments, in security-specific capacities, and in working with youths and schools. Unfortunately, there are individuals, ranging from former law enforcement officers to former educators, claiming school security expertise without ever having had responsibilities for school safety issues. Sim-

ply because someone is a former or current school administrator does not automatically qualify him or her as a school safety expert. Just because someone has a college degree does not mean that the person is automatically qualified to be a teacher or a school principal. Why then would it be assumed that someone with a degree and some type of position working in a school is automatically qualified to be a security professional?

3. *Administrators also need to check credentials.* School officials must be cautious about vague comments intended to mislead them to believe that a person has more qualifications than he or she actually does. For example, the phrases *"attended* XYZ University" or "has *a* degree from XYZ University" are vague. Did the person *graduate* from XYZ University? Is the degree a *two-year degree* or a *Ph.D.?* School officials should approach these people and organizations with caution: If someone would misrepresent himself or her organization before being hired, what would they do once a contract is signed?

4. *We must learn to scrutinize the academic answers to security problems.* There are some academicians who, unfortunately, have shifted their "research" or academic interests to fit the hot issues of the times—and to follow the money. Individuals who have had no previous interest or experience in school safety issues are now professing near overnight expertise in this area, including some who have remotely studied youth issues in other arenas and are now attempting to apply their backgrounds to school security. Some have never worked in K-12 schools, and most have never focused on school security and crisis preparedness as their full-time career. Simply because some claim that they have "studied it" or "written an article about it" does not mean that they are immediately qualified to be school security and crisis preparedness experts. Make sure that their experience reflects an understanding of K-12 school-specific security issues and needs.

5. *Experience should also have taught us to avoid product vendors for nonproduct services.* There are many sincere security vendors who want to work with schools to adapt technology to the school environment for the purpose of improving school safety. However, there are also an increasing number of vendors more concerned about breaking into the school market—and into the school budgets—with the sole purpose of making more money. School officials should scrutinize trainers and consultants to make sure that they do not misrepresent their qualifications, experience, abilities, and knowledge of school security and crisis preparedness for the purpose of selling products to their schools.

6. *Administrators also need to check the credibility, track record, experience, and references of the company and staff, specifically in the K-12 school security field.* Officials should investigate the nature of organizations providing school security and crisis preparedness resources, and should not let fancy names or titles mislead them. Is the "nonprofit" or "research" organization simply a cover for a personal consulting business? Are consultants using these titles and organizational classification in a misleading effort to enhance their credibility and convince potential clients that they are something that they are not? Are individuals associated with such legitimate organizations using them as a backdrop for their personal consulting? Are they really experts in a different area who are now adding school security to their list of alleged qualifications? These questions will help school officials make sure that companies offering school security services are truly specialized experts in this field and that slick names are not really an effort to create an appearance of enhanced legitimacy and professional interest for what is, in essence, a consulting business. A truly com-

petent, professional consulting business should be able and willing to identify itself up front. Real school security and crisis preparedness specialists should have school-specific security and crisis preparedness experience, and school-specific services to offer.

There are a number of valid questions school administrators should ask about a potential school security consultant or consulting firm before hiring them to consult or train on school security or crisis preparedness issues. These are included in Resource A, "Critical Questions in Hiring a School Security Consultant."

3

"New Times, New Crimes"
Shifts in School Security Threat Trends

We are now seeing homemade bombs, Anthrax scares, and shootings in our schools and, at the same time, there are still arguments within the education community as to whether or not we should reduce the number of open school doors because doing so might upset some staff and parents. Since we cannot agree to even this lowest level of basic security, it is not surprising that many administrators spent the months after the Columbine tragedy trying to catch up with decades of neglect in basic security and crisis preparedness measures in their schools.

Many experienced security professionals, especially school security professionals, were not overly surprised at the spate of high-profile acts of violence in American schools during 1998 and 1999. The majority of us in the field were saddened and disheartened, but not shocked. But, whereas in the past school security professionals were considered alarmists, many were now, at least for a brief period of time, suddenly looked upon as prophets and realists.

In my first book on school security (Trump, 1998), I identified the traditional top five school security concerns as

1. Aggressive and violent behavior

2. Drugs

3. Weapons

4. Gangs

5. "Stranger danger"

I also identified several emerging trends, or what I call "New times, new crimes," including

1. Bomb threats and bombs

2. Racial and cultural group conflict

3   Computer-related crimes

4. Sexual harassment and sex crimes

It is somewhat eerie to see how these four predicted growth areas, particularly the bombs and computer offenses, hit so close to home in a little over a year from the time the first book hit the market. It is equally strange to note that in less than two years from the time of publication of the book, there have already been enough significant shifts in the threat trends to revisit these issues.

Homemade Bombs and Bomb Threats

In *Practical School Security* (Trump, 1998), I noted that "school officials face a new challenge . . . with increasing domestic terrorism threats, heightened public attention to bomb scares, and easy access on the Internet to formulas for making homemade explosive devices. Bomb threats have been replaced with actual devices in school buildings and on school grounds" (p. 76). Little did I know then that this statement would hit as close to home as it did in the Columbine tragedy and the subsequent number of bomb threats and actual incidents in the months following that tragedy. It is fair to note, however, that I had been covering bombs and bomb threats as an emerging trend for over two years in our training programs, a point often dismissed then by educators in the audiences as an "alarmist" point of view.

The point is not to say, "I told you so," but I mention this to reinforce to educators that *perhaps* all school security professionals and law enforcement officials are not, as some educators have perceived the case to be, simply alarmists trying to justify their jobs. No administrator needs repeatedly to have the past thrown up in his or her face, but it is far past the time for school officials to realize that school security and school policing are, indeed, separate and distinguishable professional disciplines worthy of the respect and attention given to any other school support service. School officials must also be mindful of the importance of monitoring new trends in school security threats, because these trends tend to shift quickly over a relatively short period of time.

One in ten bomb threats might actually involve a suspicious device, but the question for most administrators is simply, "Do you want to be number ten?" Bomb threats, and now homemade bombs, must be treated seriously by school administrators. Considering the ease in getting both the formulas (from the Internet) and the ingredients (consisting of simple kitchen or household supplies) to make homemade bombs, it is likely that the potential for having such devices show up in or around school property will remain high for years to come.

Computer-Related Offenses

I also predicted in my first book that computer-related offenses would continue to present administrators with a new school security challenge. E-mailed bomb threats and death threats, along with the misuse of the Internet for finding such inappropriate materials as how-to formulas for homemade bombs, are only a couple of the new problems challenging school officials. Counterfeiting of money and hacking are the latest trends in computer misuse at home and in the schools, and such inappropriate uses of computers and technology are only likely to grow as newer technology is made more accessible to students.

A number of counterfeiting cases have already been discovered in schools. Youths are using home and school computers, scanners, color printers, and related equipment to make counterfeit money, which is often passed off in the school cafeteria to buy breakfast or lunch. Unfortunately, cafeteria workers are one of many support service groups typically left out of school training programs and staff meetings, so they often do not receive enough training in dealing with new security concerns and strategies. It is also important to stress the importance of regular supervision to computer lab teachers and other educators so that they can prevent such misuse of school technology.

Schools can also be easy targets for hackers. Although protection measures often only delay the most sophisticated computer hackers, they do deter and prevent some of the more amateur hackers from gaining access to the school computer system. Considering that items such as schedules, grades, personnel information, payroll and purchasing accounts, and other sensitive and operational materials are so readily available on computer, and that access to these and other items not only are tempting, but would also stand to cause a major disruption to school operations (not to mention a major public embarrassment) if accessed by students or other unauthorized personnel, school administrators are advised to ensure that their information systems officials build in appropriate site protection.

Internet filters and software providing the ability to track specific student use of school computers should also be used as a risk-reduction tool in school classrooms and computer labs. Individual e-mail accounts, rather than guest accounts used by potentially everyone, should be assigned to all students and staff to allow easier identification of users. Again, although these measures will not eliminate computer misuse, they will serve both as a deterrent and as tools for enhancing the ability of school and police officials to conduct investigations of misuse, if necessary.

School officials are also advised to make use of enhanced security measures for the protection of the new technology equipment itself, because this is also now a higher-risk area. If schools cannot afford an alarm system for the entire building, alarms should at least be installed in rooms with computer labs and other large-volume or high-value technology-related equipment. Whereas kids have historically broken into schools after hours, a number of cases involving adult offenders who have targeted school computer equipment have been discovered in recent years.

Although the good side of technology unquestionably outweighs the bad, school administrators who fail to recognize the potential for its misuse run the risk of becoming the subject of the next story in the local newspaper.

Weapons Shifts

The spate of school shootings in the late 1990s became the peg for political debates and intense media coverage on gun control issues, placing the focus of weapons in schools almost exclusively on firearms. In reality, firearms represent a small portion of the number of weapons confiscated in schools. In fact, according to observations from professionals in the field, the number of guns confiscated may actually be declining, although there is also a simultaneous increase in bladed weapons in schools.

Box cutters, knives, and razor blades, for example, are some of the most common types of weapons confiscated in a typical school weapon incident. It is probable that school and law enforcement officials have done such a good job in their prevention and enforcement efforts against guns in schools that they have driven youthful offenders to seek what they perceive to be a less serious form of weapon to carry and, if necessary, to use in school. Because of political agendas and media coverage slants, the focus on firearms continues, however, with bladed weapon and other weapon trends receiving little or no attention.

This is not to suggest that school violence and, in particular, weapons in schools should lead the headlines in every nightly newscast. If, however, the source of information on school weapons and other violence trends for educators is only what they see in the news, they are getting quite a skewed picture of their potential security threats and trends. The firearms-only debate, therefore, leaves the average educator looking for Johnny walking down the hallway with an automatic firearm when, in reality, Johnny may be carrying a lower-profile weapon, such as a box cutter, knife, or razor blade, any of which can be used to kill or seriously injure another student.

Educators are also very "unarmed" in terms of their training and preparedness for recognizing concealed weapons. In our workshops, I regularly ask how many of the school administrators in the audience have ever had to search a student, and inevitably the majority of participants raise their hands. Yet when they are asked how many have ever received even a brief introductory training session on identifying the various types of concealed weapons, rarely is one hand left standing in the entire room!

From a personal safety perspective, as well as from the perspective of preventing weapons from getting into the schools in general, one would think that all educators should have at least some basic awareness of the various types of concealed weapons available to students. Lipstick containers that are actually bladed weapons, knives disguised as pens, small caliber guns hidden under the soles of shoes, and razor blades hidden inside combs are only a few examples of how students can easily sneak weapons into, and carry around weapons inside of, a school. Even in schools where metal detectors are used, an untrained educator or school safety official could easily miss such items during a weapons inspection.

Gang Trends

The nature of gang activity on the streets and in schools changed noticeably across the nation in the second half of the 1990s. Some major shifts noted in our work across the country and in discussions with national gang experts include the following:

1. *A decreased use of gang identifiers.* Increased awareness of gang identifiers, such as particular clothing items, haircuts, and jewelry, by school, police, parents, and others working with youths appears to have driven such gang identification methods far underground.

2. *Increased sophistication and organization of gangs.* Gangs are increasingly organized and sophisticated in terms of not only their identification, but the methods of operation as well. A number of gangs on the street seem to be focusing their efforts on being lower profile and more clever in their operations. Some of these gangs have attempted to create a façade of legitimacy through alleged political and community activism, while others have simply employed computers, scanners, and other technology in their operations. Gang connections between correctional institution members and those on the streets are also as strong as ever, if not stronger, according to various specialists in the field. At the school and in the younger aged gang members on the streets, their lower profile, increased mobility, and constantly shifting leadership and membership have also made it quite difficult to identify and track them and their gangs.

3. *Decreased gang statistics, changes in reporting, and elimination or reduction in official responses.* The factors described above and others have led to increased difficulty in distinguishing gang members from non–gang member offenders and, in essence, in identifying the organization, leadership, and structure of the gangs. The absence of such recognition and identification has led to the official perception by many school, law enforcement, and political officials that the gang presence and associated problems have gone away and no longer exist simply because they cannot see them as clearly as they could in the past. It has also led to decreased gang statistics in police and other organizations attempting to collect such data, and this absence of data further fuels the perception that the problem, or the potential for a problem, no longer exists. Field observations suggest that the level of gang activity may have subsided from its real and perceived climbs in the early 1990s; however, this leveling off and inability to see gangs as clearly has also led to the reduction or elimination of gang enforcement and prevention efforts in a number of schools and communities.

Several gang specialists, including myself, predict that several things will occur in the gang arena as we enter the millennium:

1. Anticipated growth of the juvenile population in the middle years of the first millennium decade will also see a resurrection of gang activity and a growth of juvenile crime problems in general.

2. Gang member sophistication, organization, and mobility will continue to grow, as will the misuse of technology by gangs. The number of gang, drug, and associated crimes using the Internet and other forms of computers and technology is highly likely to grow. A growing gang member presence in legitimate organizations, such as businesses, the military, public safety agencies, and perhaps even some positions within schools, will likely be experienced. The more sophisticated gangs may also explore expanded involvement in political activities and misuse of the media, including associated efforts to influence school political and administrative bodies.

3. Gangs will continue to reflect demographic changes in our society, with Asian, Latino, and other minority populations continuing to experience an increased presence of gang affiliation within their cultures. Likewise, white supremacy gangs, antigovernment groups, racial conflicts, and hate crimes will also likely continue to grow in number and in sophistication. Female gang involvement, and corresponding female arrests and incarceration, will likely continue to grow.

4. The cycle of gang denial, acknowledgment, and action in many communities will continue to shift back to denial and a qualified admittance until major demographic changes and other dynamics bring the issue back to the forefront sometime around the year 2005. Gang enforcement, prevention, and intervention progress will therefore continue to suffer setbacks until community leaders cycle back out of denial, and the problems become so severe that they can no longer be denied or covered up.

The shift of gang activity to forms that are lower in profile and more organized presents school officials with an even greater problem than that which they had when gang activity in and around school was more overt. Although the overt activity still exists in schools, oftentimes spilling over from community conflicts, educators are finding it increasingly difficult to identify gang members and to prevent potential problems until after violence has erupted. The importance of ongoing training for school officials, and for their networking with school and public safety specialists, will likely never be greater than it will be in upcoming years.

Terrorist Targets?

Attention to international and domestic terrorism in the late 1990s should lead us to question how vulnerable our schools might be to terrorist attacks and threats. There is no question that Americans overall are sensitive to the impact of violence and that the acts of terrorists shock even the most veteran public safety officials. The shock value of terrorist threats and acts is multiplied when children are involved.

What would you do if your school received an Anthrax scare? What if a gunman upset with the government enters your school and takes several staff and students hostage? Or, what if a school is bombed by international terrorists as their means of sending a message to U.S. leaders? Although these questions raise horrible thoughts, the reality of such incidents occurring would be even more horrible. To avoid thinking about preventing and managing such terrorist attacks, however, would be most horrible, if not negligent. School officials must realize that violence is not pretty and that they need to prepare for the worst-case scenario, even though it might never occur.

Still, although we hope that it will never occur, the sad reality is that this may be one of the next waves of violence to hit our schools.

Adult-Originated Violence

School officials often focus only on security threats that originate from youths. Many times this youth threat is perceived as being only from the inside (i.e., from students) or the outside (i.e., from nonstudent trespassers). Not only should the youth threats be anticipated from both inside and outside of the school, but educators should also recognize adult-originated security threats.

Irate Parents

Many principals view dealing with irate parents as a given part of their job, but the potential volatility of irate parents is increasingly leaving a number of school administrators concerned about their safety and the safety of staff and students. Alcohol, drug, and mental health problems experienced by some parents further enhance the risks some administrators must face.

School officials need to be cognizant of potential irate parent situations and, when possible, to take such preventive measures as organizing a parent conference when they perceive a risk. Educators also need to remember the importance of greeting and questioning parents whom they know by sight or who may even be in the building on a daily basis, because the moods, influences, and motivations of these individuals could change due to circumstances. Educators might think that they know these parent "regulars," but they may not necessarily know if that person is under the influence of mind-altering substances that day, if they are angry at a particular staff member, or if there are family conflicts being brought into the school unless those educators communicate with the parents and ascertain their purpose during each visit.

Noncustodial parents also present safety concerns for school officials, most commonly at the elementary level. Rarely do we find an elementary school where there are not, or have not been, concerns about parents wanting to remove or potentially to harm children who are not in their legal custody. Discrete communications between key staff and proper follow-through with related policies are critical to ensuring student and staff safety.

Workplace Violence

Working for a school district can be a wonderful experience. Working with children can be quite rewarding. However, it can also be quite stressful. Added to this normal amount of stress is the fact that school districts are, in essence, government and political entities. Not only is the school bureaucracy a world of its own in many districts, but so, too, is the world of school politics. Some of the most unique personalities and political games that I have ever come across have been within school districts across the nation.

One need not look too far into this picture to see the perfect formula for workplace violence: workload stress from the youths, plus bureaucracy stress and political stress. It is somewhat surprising that there have not been more incidents of workplace violence by disgruntled school employees, considering the amount of adult-driven stress and the political games played with individuals and their careers. As school districts continue to become increasingly politicized and stressed, from the boardrooms to the classrooms and custodial offices, we can anticipate a growing potential for workplace violence.

Domestic Spillover

The spillover of domestic conflicts from staff and parent homes should also be considered in developing crisis guidelines. Serious conflicts between spouses, where at least one spouse is a school employee, or by parents of students can easily be continued on school grounds or in school buildings. Administrators need to be aware of potential related crime and violence ranging from vandalism to vehicles all the way to murder.

Such conflicts present administrators with a difficult situation, because these matters are perceived both by the participants and by school employees as being personal. The none-of-your-business attitude might be appropriate as long as the conflict does not affect the school setting, but when it comes to the school, or has a potential to come to the school, then the antagonism does, to some extent, become the school officials' business. Administrators need to be attuned to such problems, and they need to ensure that their staff and parents feel comfortable in giving them a heads-up warning of potential problems.

Teen Suicide and Self-Harm

Suicide and other self-harm threats and attempts have been made in schools long before the recent high-profile school violence cases. Although educators need to give serious attention to all such threats, they should reasonably anticipate that the schools might become a more popular place, because there has been so much media and public attention to violence at schools in recent years, for students thinking about committing such acts to carry out their plans. After all, if an individual is seeking attention, where else would he or she be more likely to believe that such an act would become known by the most individuals than if it is committed at school?

Sexual Harassment, Sex Crimes, and Drug Offenses

The potential for sex and drug offenses to continue at their current rates—if not at increased rates—is rather high. These problems have always plagued our communities and, to varying degrees, our schools. There is no indication that either type of offense will decline in the long term, although it is probable that both will continue to rise in the near future because of the continued growth of social, economic, and especially psychological ills driving these crimes.

Conversations with many students suggest that the problem of peer sexual harassment may be more pervasive than many adults believe or care to acknowledge. Sexual comments, improper touching, and related harassment are daily occurrences in many schools. In some cases, school staff have appeared oblivious to such actions, suggesting that this inappropriate behavior may, by default, be accepted as a part of "normal" student behavior.

Drug trends vary from community to community and from time to time within the same community. Unfortunately, many educators do not take advantage of available local resources, such as having police officers assigned to the school, working with crime prevention officers within police departments, or having police representatives provide periodic briefings to school staff on drug recognition and trends in the community. Schools reflect their communities, and to think that schools are untouched by drug activity within the broader community is a naive and unrealistic belief.

Bullying, Fights, and Other Aggressive Behavior

It is also important to remember that bullying, verbal conflicts, physical assaults, and related aggressive behaviors are still the most common forms of school violence across the nation. I believe strongly that these lower-level forms of violence are truly the red flags for the more serious and sophisticated offenses that often follow. Dealing with small problems while they are small will likely keep school officials from having to deal with bigger problems that arise because they neglected the small conflicts in their early stages.

Bullying is one of the earliest and most prevalent forms of school violence. A "boys will be boys" or "girls will be girls" mentality by adults will only exacerbate the problem. Today's bully is often tomorrow's gang member or other violent youthful offender. If educators are sincere about prevention, they will start looking at the presence of bullying, attempt to minimize it while children are at a very young age, and consistently reinforce related prevention and intervention strategies as these children grow through their school-age years.

Will the Gap Widen?

School officials, like any other public safety agency, will always be behind in terms of keeping up with the offenders. The question, though, is how far will they allow the gap between the ever-changing criminal techniques of youthful offenders and the preparedness of educators to prevent and manage such offenses to widen? Reasonable risk reduction and crisis preparation measures are critical to keeping this gap small and manageable.

Unfortunately, schools have done a poor job over recent decades by allowing the gap to widen far beyond what it should ever have been allowed to reach. Although challenged by such "new times, new crimes" problems as homemade bombs, technology offenses, and terroristic threats, most schools are only now reaching the point of discussing whether or not to reduce the number of doors left open to the school. Denial, image concerns, politics, and the lack of understanding of professional school security and crisis preparedness strategies have all contributed to the current state where many educators are attempting to catch up overnight for decades of neglect in even the most basic security and crisis preparedness measures.

It is obvious that, when we can walk through only a limited number of open doors at a fast food restaurant and are greeted by someone, yet the doors in our schools are wide open and nobody challenges a stranger's presence, our schools are underprepared and we must work to change this. We must move quickly, but thoroughly and methodically, to close the gap between school security threats and their appropriate countermeasures. If not, educators will be found continuing to scratch their heads in amazement when the next tragedy strikes.

4

Early Warning Signs
Fact, Fiction, or Fad?

The number of gurus and gadgets popping up to "help" educators improve school safety skyrocketed in the late 1990s, especially following the violence at Columbine High School in April of 1999. There are now various checklists, software, and consultants who have the "answer" to help schools identify and prevent potentially violent offenders. The key is finding a balance between recognizing the red flags of potential violence that should raise educators' eyebrows while still exercising care and caution to avoid inappropriate labeling and misidentifica- tion of children.

Are there children who are ticking time bombs ready to explode with violent behavior in our schools and in our communities? School violence incidents have led many people to ask if there are early warning signs indicating the potential for violent behaviors by youths, and many opinions have subsequently been offered on the subject. Although most professionals agree that there are some red flags that should, at a minimum, raise some adult eyebrows as to a child's potential for involvement in violence, agreement upon what those flags actually look like and how they should be identified is much less common.

Concerns and Caveats

Following the series of school violence tragedies in the late 1990s, a number of checklists, computer software programs, overnight expert consultants, and other "resources" appeared to "help" school officials and others identify potentially violent offenders before an actual incident. One computer program reportedly analyzed student essays for the purpose of identifying violent words that would indicate a potentially violent student. Heaven help the poor child who writes an essay on war!

In one workshop on school crisis preparedness, I spoke with two principals who were looking at a checklist of "common characteristics" of potentially violent youthful offenders. One administrator commented, "Over 90% of my student population fits this list of characteristics, but I don't believe that 90% of them are very likely to shoot up or blow up our school." The other administrator responded: "And I can't think of one kid in my school who fits this so-called profile, but I can think of about a half-dozen kids who I'm sure are higher risk for bringing in anything they can get their hands on and destroying all of us!"

An understanding of youth and delinquent psychology can unquestionably help parents, school officials, and other youth service providers to better deal with potentially violent youths. However, the explosion of overnight expert consultants, checklists, software programs, and other profiling mechanisms following school violence incidents has, in a sense, created some dilemmas in addressing the entire issue of recognizing early warning signs of potentially violent youths. Particular concerns include these:

1. *Parents, school officials, and other youth service providers placed in the role of pseudo-psychologists.* Psychology and counseling are professions that require extensive training, certification, and other professional preparation. Lists of early warning signs and other products need to be viewed within an appropriate context and in a reasonable manner. Authoring a checklist does not automatically make someone an expert in psychology. When a red flag pops up, educators and others should remember to consult with professionals, such as licensed psychologists or counselors, when concerns arise.

2. *Misuse of early warning sign resources.* Caution should be exercised not to allow checklists or computer software programs to be used to stereotype or classify children, or to over- or underreact to the potential for youth violence. Some schools may have a large number of children with characteristics on an early warning sign list, yet none of them will commit a violent, tragic act. Other schools may have children who show none of the characteristics on such a guide, yet one may commit a violent offense. Lists and other products need to be viewed within an appropriate context and in a reasonable manner.

3. *Unwarranted fears that only "experts" can effectively identify and work with high-risk youths.* Media and public attention to school violence incidents may unintentionally communicate to parents, educators, and others that only highly trained "experts" can have an impact with high-risk youths. Although an understanding of, and increased training on, youth and delinquent behavior can be quite helpful and is to be encouraged, parents and others who work with children should not resign themselves to inaction because they do not have a degree in abnormal psychology or counseling! Such a paralysis of adults can only contribute to youth violence by driving the average parent or teacher away from the children, not closer where they need to be to help control and prevent it.

Checklists, Software, and Gurus

I believe that there are behavioral indicators that should serve as red flags for adults in terms of recognizing that there is at least the potential that they might be dealing with a youth at a higher level of risk for committing violence. However, I am also concerned about the use, and potential for misuse, of various so-called checklists and similar products being produced in response to this issue. Some questions that need to be asked when these lists, software products, and similar "resources" are offered include the following:

- Who made the checklists or software program, and what are their qualifications and perspectives in doing so? Have they ever worked on a full-time basis with youths, violent juvenile offenders, and K-12 school safety issues?

- Who will use these checklists or software programs, and in what context? Will everyone, from the custodian to the superintendent, be checking off lists to profile potentially violent kids? Is the profile limited to self-reports by the student or to the perspective of the profiler? What about parent and family input?

- What will be done once these items are used? Assuming that you have a valid reference tool and qualified people to use it, what will be done with a potentially violent offender once he or she is identified? What services are available, and how are they engaged and sustained? What do you do if the parents and/or the child refuse services? Does the school have, or even want to have, a policy mandating evaluation before a child can attend school?

These and a number of other issues need to be examined closely before using checklists, software programs, and other products and services.

The Profiling Paradox

The emergence of various checklists and software products following the late-1990s school shootings stirred up a number of media, conference, and other professional debates around concerns of labeling or misidentifying children as potentially violent offenders. The debates and polarization grew even stronger following the publication of an article in the September issue of *FBI Law Enforcement Bulletin* (Band & Harpold, 1999) that included sections on violence indicators, and in particular an offender profile, in connection with the school shootings of previous years. A number of professionals, especially educators, questioned everything from the validity of the offender profile to the expertise and appropriateness of the FBI having involvement in the school violence arena.

According to the article, the FBI's involvement began when they moderated an August 1998 two-day school violence summit held in Arkansas with representatives from six cities that had experienced recent school shootings.

The lessons learned from the shooting were summarized in the article and in presentations made by FBI officials to school and law enforcement personnel in various conferences across the country the following year. Although a number of issues in the lessons learned covered logistical and coordination preparation suggestions, public and media attention seemed to focus strongly on the profiling aspect; that is, on suggestions that the FBI was teaching educators how to profile potentially violent offenders.

In the September 1999 article, the agents identified several factors "that may indicate that individuals have the potential to commit violence" (p. 13), including

- Low self-esteem
- Previous acts of cruelty to animals
- Fascination with firearms
- Disrespect from mothers or other family members
- Seeing violence as the only alternative left for them

Although these indicators were made with several references to the six school shootings, the article did indicate that they were "by no means certain or present in every case of violence" (p. 13).

Probably even more controversial was the title and concept behind the article's offender profile section. Here, the agents indicated that the suspects from the six shootings displayed similar traits, including that they

- Were white males under 18 years old with mass- or spree-murder traits
- Sought to defend narcissistic views or favorable views about themselves
- Experienced an event prior to their acts that resulted in depression and suicidal thoughts turning homicidal
- Had or perceived a lack of family support, and felt rejected and wronged by others
- Had a history of mental health treatment
- Were influenced by satanic or cult-type beliefs
- Listened to songs that promoted violence
- Appeared isolated and felt powerless
- Openly expressed a desire to kill, an interest in previous killings, and had no remorse after the killings

The agents again qualified this section by noting that "any one of these characteristics alone may not describe a potential school shooter," although they did add that, "taken together, they provide a profile that may assist law enforcement, schools, and communities to identify at-risk students" (p. 14).

I strongly suspect that the connotation of the word *profile* in itself triggered a number of strong feelings leading to the voicing of concern regarding the FBI's involvement in the school safety issue. General public opinion and a number of news stories claiming that law enforcement authorities were using race to profile highway drivers for traffic stops in order to conduct drug searches received high-profile attention around this same time, making the word *profile* automatically mean "racial profiling" or "suspected drugs" in the eyes of a number of citizens. This, in itself, appeared to be reason enough for some automatically to dismiss the points raised in the FBI article and other public discussions on the topic.

It is also arguable not only that the FBI's involvement stemmed from their interest in taking a leadership role by gleaning some commonality from the various incidents, but that their higher profile in doing so could easily have been driven from higher up in the federal government where political pressures existed to initiate some highly visible efforts. Doing so would give the federal government something visible to point to in terms of their efforts to stop school shootings, which many people felt were out of control. What better claim could a politician or political appointee make, when challenged by reporters or their political foes, than saying, "We even have the FBI working on these issues. What more can we do?" After seeing a number of federal law enforcement retirees cited in the media after the shootings as "school safety experts," some other observers privately went so far as to suggest that perhaps some current federal law enforcement officials might also have a secondary agenda: that of casting themselves as experts in this area to position themselves for post-retirement jobs as school security directors or consultants.

Regardless of possible political and individual agendas, the collection and dissemination of information on common themes from the high profile incidents is indeed a worthy project. In regard to the FBI's involvement, credit should be given to a number of their field offices for taking a leadership role in bringing such information to school and law enforcement officials within their region. In fact, when reviewing the agendas for several of their sponsored presentations, two of which I participated in directly, I found their efforts to be quite sincere in terms of assembling established professionals with firsthand experience and expertise in their respective presentation areas. So, to characterize all of these efforts as being politically driven or grandstanding efforts would be unfair.

Early Warning, Timely Response

Following a number of the high-profile school shootings, the U.S. Departments of Education and Justice published a document titled, *Early Warning, Timely Response: A Guide to Safe Schools* (Dwyer, Osher, & Warger, 1998) in an effort to "develop an early warning guide to help adults reach out to troubled children quickly and effectively" (Riley & Reno, 1998, p. 1). The guide focuses on a number of safe schools perspectives, including characteristics of safe schools, getting help for children, and developing prevention and crisis response plans. The section on early warning signs, however, appears to have captured the most public attention.

The authors appropriately indicated early on in the document the potential dangers of misinterpreting these identified signs, and they encouraged readers not to use the publication as a checklist for labeling or stereotyping children. They also stressed that violence and aggression must be viewed and understood within environmental and developmental contexts. By placing a number of qualifying statements in the publication to avoid misunderstandings and misuse, the authors professionally and responsibly presented complex information in a clear and useful manner.

Early warning signs were presented in the report with the stipulation that all signs are not equally significant, that the items were not presented in the text in order of seriousness, and that it is inappropriate and potentially harmful to use the signs alone as an index for predicting aggression and violence. The authors also noted that troubled children typically exhibit multiple warning signs and that this often occurs repeatedly and with increasing intensity over a period of time. With these qualifiers, the authors presented a series of early warning signs, which includes

- Social withdrawal
- Excessive feelings of isolation and being alone
- Excessive feelings of rejection
- Being a victim of violence
- Feelings of being picked on and persecuted
- Low school interest and poor academic performance
- Expression of violence in writings and drawings
- Uncontrolled anger
- Patterns of impulsive and chronic hitting, intimidation, and bullying behaviors
- A history of discipline problems
- A history of violent and aggressive behavior
- Intolerance for differences and prejudicial attitudes
- Drug use and alcohol use
- Affiliation with gangs
- Inappropriate access to, possession of, and use of firearms
- Serious threats of violence

The authors distinguished these early warning signs from what they called "imminent warning signs," which indicate a greater potential for a student to behave in a potentially dangerous manner and which require an immediate response. These signs include

- Serious physical fighting with peers or family members
- Severe destruction of property
- Severe rage for seemingly minor reasons
- Detailed threats of lethal violence
- Possession and/or use of firearms and other weapons

- Other self-injurious behaviors or threats of suicides

The authors stressed that safety must be the first priority and that action must be taken immediately when these signs exist. They also stressed the importance of notifying parents and involving law enforcement if detailed plans to cause harm, a history of aggression or previous attempts to carry out threats, or possession of a weapon and threats to use it have occurred.

Frontline Observations

Based on over 15 years of work in the school safety and youth violence fields, my wife (a social worker and former juvenile probation officer) and I pulled together a number of psychosocial and behavioral indicators and themes that we have observed from the front lines in dealing firsthand with some of the most violent young offenders on our streets. These observations are simply that: observations. They are not the result of formal research and, although a number of them appear to be consistent with both research and the positions of a number of other established professionals discussing these issues, they are presented here simply to illustrate that we have observed, at least in our professional experiences, a number of red flags that should alert individuals living and working with potentially violent youths of possible trouble.

The same qualifying factors presented by the authors of *Early Warning, Timely Response* (Dwyer et al., 1998) most certainly apply to our observations. They should not be used as a checklist or profile by educators or other youth-serving professionals to predict violence or aggression. They also should be viewed within environmental and developmental contexts. We agree that the presence of multiple psychosocial and/or behavioral indicators and an increase in frequency and intensity of behavioral indicators should be noted—and a great deal of common sense must be applied—by those processing this entire issue to avoid mislabeling or misidentifying youths.

In addition to the various indicators, an equally strong emphasis must be placed on what is actually done once particular psychosocial or behavioral indicators are identified. As I noted above, we view these as red flags to alert individuals, who are not trained and licensed mental health professionals, that there may be a need to seek more in-depth assistance from such professionals. In other words, the various potential indicators discussed in this chapter should be the triggers for seeking professional help, not tools for making individuals who are non-mental health professionals into something they are not qualified to be.

Stressors and Coping Factors

A variety of social and economic factors can contribute to violent and aggressive behavior by children at home, in school, and in the community. In cases of workplace violence, we tend to look at the offenders to identify what stressors led them to commit violent acts. Ironically, we tend not to look at our juvenile population from the same perspective, particularly in terms of thinking about prevention and the early recognition of warning signs.

Children, especially teens, are influenced by numerous stress factors. We believe that youth stressors and coping factors deserve a place in our discussions of youth and school violence. Our observations have found some of the more common stressors to include, but not necessarily be limited to, the following:

- Physical, psychological, and/or emotional abandonment by parents, adults, and significant others
- Domestic violence, abuse, neglect, and/or other severe family stress or dysfunction
- Lack of order, structure, and discipline
- Self-concept formation, peer pressure, the need to protect reputation, and related developmental issues
- Alcohol, drug, and similar influences
- Gang, cult, or other deviant subculture attraction
- Pressure to succeed academically and/or to meet parental expectations (real or perceived)
- Fear of the unknown, fear of rejection, and fear of failure

These and other influences leave our children with an enormous amount of stress and internal conflict that might contribute toward triggering aggressive and violent behavior. Nevertheless, such stressors in themselves are very common, so the use of these stress factors as a checklist for profiling potentially violent offenders would be stretching it quite a bit, because many, if not all, youths might experience these stressors at one point or another, especially during their teen years.

Knowing that these pressures exist and that some children, especially teens, may lack adequate and appropriate coping skills for dealing with them is important. Perhaps the focus should be on the presence or absence of coping skills and support mechanisms, along with identifying what triggers the transition from stressor to violent behavior, rather than just the presence or absence of the stress characteristics alone. It is reasonable, then, to say that we are almost automatically dealing with a higher-risk population simply because they are teenagers, and in working with them we should have a heightened awareness (but not fear or panic) of the importance of being attuned to stress and related coping issues.

Behavioral and Psychosocial Observations

We looked back over 15 years at the hundreds of violent youthful offenders we have dealt with in urban and suburban settings, which included the some of the most hard-core gang members, drug traffickers, and aggressive youths at elementary and secondary school levels, as well as those outside of school settings. The most common behavioral and psychosocial indicators and themes we observed are listed below. These are not ranked in terms of seriousness or frequency of our observations.

- Poor interpersonal skills
- Lack of trust, bonding, and relationships
- Impulsiveness, spontaneity, an addiction to excitement, and a high need for instant gratification
- Strong focus on receiving respect and the need to protect one's reputation
- Very short-term focus with no vision of a future and a distrust of long-range commitments
- Early and lengthy history of substance abuse
- Sexual activity, particularly at younger ages and with multiple consenting partners, or with pressured and unwilling partners
- Unmet physical and/or mental health needs
- Poor educational and/or employment performance
- Functioning well in negative subcultures, often with high self-esteem in that arena, along with effective use of survival skills, a strong drive for goals (typically negative goals), and an intense affiliation to the subculture
- Skilled at negotiations and very manipulative
- Competitive, seeks challenges, and is action-oriented
- Strong need for approval and adult status

As previously stated, it is important that these characteristics not be viewed as a checklist, *per se*. Readers should also understand that one or more characteristic alone is generally less likely to raise major red flags. However, clusters of the behavioral responses described in this chapter, especially when these responses increase in frequency or intensity to particular triggers or stimuli, understandably justify further attention and probable referral for more professional mental health attention.

Similar to the imminent warning signs mentioned in *Early Warning, Timely Response* (Dwyer et al., 1998), the following indicators raise our red flags very quickly and heighten the urgency of providing professional mental health services:

- Suicidal thoughts or attempts, and related self-injury and harm
- Attempting to cause the death of or serious physical harm to another
- Intentional abuse of animals
- Setting fires
- Hallucinations or other delusions
- Specific plans, especially detailed ones, for committing violence

Again, red flags should indicate the need to seek help from mental health professionals specifically experienced in working with troubled, violent youths. These signs are not intended to represent a diagnostic checklist or tool for laypersons to use to draw clinical conclusions or as the sole deciding factor for specific administrative, disciplinary, or criminal action in connection with an individual student.

A Continuum of Aggression and Violence

Although the initial public accounts of school shootings or other youth violence may suggest that the violent acts came totally unexpected and without warning, the picture typically changes as the story unravels. Days, weeks, or months later, it is not uncommon for a progressive series of behavioral deterioration in the offender to become more visible. In short, the circumstances behind these high-profile events rarely develop overnight.

References to increases in frequency and intensity of violence have been made in several sections of this chapter. Perhaps the movement from lower levels of aggression to higher-profile violence is best characterized using the framework of the spectrum of aggressive behavior (Silver & Yudofsky, 1992). This spectrum or continuum includes

- Verbal aggression, ranging from shouting and insults to clear threats of violence
- Physical aggression against objects, including property damage, fire setting, and similar harm to inanimate objects
- Physical aggression against self, including physical self-harm, mutilation, or suicidal behavior
- Physical aggression against others, such as assaults and serious physical injury or death to others

Although every situation may not be traceable to a systematic move through these stages, there are often indicators associated with progression through this spectrum that tend to be missed until "armchair quarterbacking" is performed on higher-profile incidents.

Consideration of behavioral and psychosocial indicators alone will only provide a portion of the available insight into a youth's mental health world. An analysis of other environmental and contextual influences provide other important pieces of information for assessing a youth's behavior and related violence concerns.

Youth Supervision and Discipline

It is not uncommon to hear people from all walks of life blaming parents, school officials, and other adults associated with violent youthful offenders for allowing a lack of discipline and supervision to exist, which, in people's opinions, caused a violent behavior. In our years of observations with violent youths, we have found the following related themes:

- Inconsistent presence of parental authority figures
- Inconsistent discipline or extremes in terms of too little or too much discipline for a particular situation

- Parent-child role reversals, where the child often seems to be in control rather than the other way around
- Youths who are confident that there will be no timely and appropriate consequences for negative behavior
- Minimal supervision of or ineffective limits of control over a youth
- The youth's minimal basic needs beyond mere physical survival are not met

Although discipline and supervision alone may not be the only factors playing into violent youthful behavior, the presence of firm, fair, and consistent discipline and supervision certainly reduces the risks.

Family Stress and Dysfunction

Stress, dysfunction, and related dynamics within the family unquestionably play a major role in influencing a youth's behavior. Common themes observed in families of the violent children with whom we have worked have included the following:

- Physical, sexual, and/or emotional abuse
- Domestic violence, intimidation, and/or viewing significant others as objects and, therefore, as less human
- Parental abandonment, either physically and/or emotionally, due to divorce or separation, parental incarceration, parental mental health problems, parental substance use/abuse, parental physical health problems, or parental work obligations, all of which may draw attention to other lifestyle or household management issues while detracting from the attention to youth needs and behavior
- Feelings of rejection due to parental alcohol or drug abuse, mental health issues, criminal history, and/or incarceration
- Unstable residences or caretakers
- Lack of defined family and/or family boundaries
- Abused siblings, neglected siblings, or siblings involved in crime and violence

Again, these factors do not necessarily predict violent youthful behavior in themselves, but they should be recognized as possible contributing factors, especially when they are one of a cluster of conditions.

Youth Worker Characteristics

The tendency to look at youths, their families, and related dynamics often fails to include an examination of the characteristics of the individuals who are working with the youth and how these characteristics are sometimes counterproductive to reducing risks of youth violence and adverse behavior. Some particular observations we have made over the years include the tendency of many youth workers and youth-serving organizations and systems to be

- Rigid, bureaucratic, and restricted in operations and service delivery
- Traditional, predictable, and routine in terms of what the youth can expect of the workers and the system
- Demanding, pushing the youth to adapt to a system that might not be designed or operated in a manner that meets the youth's issues and needs
- Delivering services from a worker's point of view, without consideration of how the youth and his or her significant others define and perceive their issues and needs
- Unreasonable in expecting immediate trust, bonding, and relationships with the client youths and families
- Unreasonable in seeking and expecting quick progress and success, often failing to realize that they are attempting to undo years of adverse behavior patterns in a relatively short period of time, which often leads them to terminate or alter services too quickly or inappropriately because they perceive an absence of progress or change

This is not to suggest that the workers or the systems are solely to blame for youth violence or the failure of youths to change behavioral directions. It is, however, meant to suggest that those adults working with youths need to take their perspective, and the perspective of their own organization and its service delivery, into consideration when evaluating individual cases.

A Holistic Assessment

It should be clear from the preceding sections of this chapter that individuals attempting to look for early warning signs to determine whether a referral for more professional mental health assistance is needed cannot simply rely on a checklist. Instead, they need to consider a variety of areas of youth functioning. These may include paying attention to

- Behavior changes at home, including in relationships with parents and siblings
- The general mood and attitude of the youth (e.g., psychological state, depression, etc.)
- Physical signs, such as medical needs, physical injuries, illness, and personal hygiene
- Social changes in terms of peer relationships, how peer conflicts are managed, activities the youth is engaged in, and any significant changes
- School performance
- Work performance

- Family history, including issues of substance use and abuse, domestic violence, sexual abuse, physical abuse, emotional abuse, and mental illness
- Legal/court involvement
- Sexuality
- Family residential stability (e.g., mobility, transitions, etc.)
- Changes in family economic status or needs
- The loss of loved one through death, separation, or abandonment
- Other trauma or the concerns of others knowledgeable about the youth

Although many people, especially educators, enjoy the checklist approach to addressing issues, human behavior and, in particular, youth behavior and violence are simply not that easy. Unlike many adults, who are often set in their ways, "normal" youth behavior is very experimental, and therefore can change for an ongoing period of time, particularly during adolescence. If we agree that attempts to accurately profile adults are long shots, then it should be clear that such an approach is even more difficult when applied to children and teens.

Prevention, Intervention, and Treatment Issues

Parents and Educators

Parents, school officials, and other youth service providers can take numerous steps to reduce the stressors on children and, in turn, to help lower the risks of stress-triggered violent behavior. Some of these steps might include the following:

1. Establish ongoing, sincere, and trusting relationships with youths built on regular, quality communications.

2. Be sensitive to the stressors influencing children and provide timely intervention support.

3. Be alert for, and promptly respond to, such issues as

- Detachment or a lack of bonding and connectedness to others
- Withdrawal or perceptions of hopelessness
- Threats—and the efforts to establish the means and opportunity to carry out the threats
- Disciplinary problems in school and/or delinquent, criminal activity in schools or communities
- Unusual interest or preoccupation with weapons, bombs, violent entertainment forms (e.g., music, movies, etc.)
- Abuse of animals, suicide threats or attempts, self-mutilation, etc.

4. Be consistent in expectations and in disciplining youths.

5. Listen to kids with a nonjudgmental attitude, even if you disagree with their perspectives. The emphasis is on listening, not on having to agree with what you hear.

6. Be alert to small, incremental changes in youth behavior instead of waiting for *the* major event. The importance of looking at *changes* in behavior, rather than for a specific list of behaviors, cannot be overstated. And to be able to detect a change in behavior, adults working with youths first need to know what is standard behavior for that child before they can detect a change. In other words, you will be less likely to detect a change in Johnny's behavior on Friday if you do not know what Johnny's typical behavior is on Monday, Tuesday, Wednesday, and Thursday. Although this does not easily lend itself to those who prefer a checklist or cookie-cutter approach to dealing with kids, it does provide an accurate depiction of reality, in that the key to dealing with at-risk youths and preventing youth and school violence rests strongly in knowing and working with children as individuals.

Parents and professionals working with youths should especially remember to talk with children honestly and, when necessary, to seek professional help *before* a situation reaches a crisis level. Dealing with small concerns is a much more manageable task than dealing with crises.

Professional and Program Considerations

Like any professionals who work with violent youths, my wife and I have developed some basic beliefs about how prevention, intervention, and treatment for such youths should be approached. These beliefs include, but are not necessarily limited to, the need

- To focus on individualized approaches to at-risk and violent youths, instead of using cookie-cutter approaches and programs for all
- To recognize that multiple attempts may very well need to be made with the same kid before progress is seen
- For individuals working with youths to attempt to understand, even if they do not agree with, the logic and thinking of the youth as he or she views issues, needs, or concerns
- For a commitment to skilled interviewing and communications with youths in terms of recognizing the need to check multiple sources of information (not simply the child or a particular adult), the tendency of youths to answer questions literally or in a very narrow and specific manner, and the tendency of many youths to exaggerate, minimize, or rationalize behaviors
- For continuous monitoring, supervision, and support
- For simple, direct, and concrete communications to be made when setting rules and expectations
- For firmness, fairness, and consistency, with an emphasis on order and structure, in discipline and supervision

- To engage constructive, and sometimes new, methods for youths to cope with stress, conflict, and related dynamics
- To focus on building and maintaining long-term relationships, which are often absent, but are needed, in many violence-prone youths
- For strong drug prevention, education, and employment plans, which are necessary to keep youths in the direction of progress
- To recognize that even the most violent youths may be clever, creative, skillful, and manipulative—in either a positive or a negative manner depending upon the circumstances
- To address concretely issues of self-respect, respect for others, and dealing with challenges to respect
- To acknowledge that youths, and especially at-risk or violence-prone youths, often require meaningful challenges, mental and physical stimulation, exposure to new areas, and involvement in the planning and process for prevention, intervention, and/or treatment
- To emphasize meaningful and useful short-term tasks, along with immediate and tangible payoffs and feedback, which may be the most successful approach to dealing with at-risk or violence-prone youths
- To recognize that youths—and adults—must learn patience with the process, and to acknowledge the importance of long-term goals in addition to the short-term issues
- For youths to understand and distinguish between the short- and long-term consequences of adverse behavior
- For youths (and for that matter, many adults, too) to learn to differentiate wants from needs
- For youths to be able to recognize negative behavior in others (including in their role models), to evaluate the depth of their "friendships" with and the motivations of others, and to respond appropriately
- For a balance of rights with responsibilities
- To include social skills issues in working with at-risk or violence-prone youths, and to focus on teaching youths how to ask for help and assistance, manage embarrassment, deal with disrespect, and handle rumors, change, and related concerns

Another Call for Common Sense

Psychology, mental health, crime, violence, and aggression are all very complex issues. Although we cannot bypass or look only at the surface of these issues and expect that we will not miss some major warning signs, we also do not need "paralysis by analysis" to the point where we believe that only individuals with doctoral degrees and dozens of years experience in a mental health profession can detect potential initial indicators of violence. In fact, I truly fear that the extensive media coverage of school and youth violence in the 1990s has led many parents, teachers, and others who work with kids to fear that, because the issues are so complex, they simply cannot recognize some early warning signs, and that therefore they simply will not bother trying to do so.

The reality is that good observation skills and common sense can alert many adults to impending problems. For example, art and English teachers are in excellent positions to detect early warning signs of potentially violent youths by looking closely at their drawings, essays, and related projects for themes of violence. Common sense should indicate that if the project is on war, then the project may reasonably include such themes, but if projects show in-depth themes of violence, especially on an ongoing basis, then it might be a good idea to refer concerns to a school counselor, psychologist, or administrator.

In the end, common sense and a heightened awareness of early warning signs, combined with timely and appropriate follow-through, can help prevent school and other youth violence tragedies while avoiding inappropriate labeling and misidentification of youths as violent offenders.

II

Applying the Lessons Learned

The school violence tragedies of the late 1990s have permanently changed the face of school safety across the nation. A shift from prevention- and intervention-only approaches to a multitude of school security and crisis preparedness strategies came about nearly overnight in many schools and communities. Academic, political, media, and other public debates from all perspectives focused on lessons learned from the tragedies on how to make schools safe.

This section of the book applies the lessons raised in the previous section, as well as a number of other new school security and crisis preparedness strategies. Considerations for assessing and managing student threats, establishing a framework for reducing safety risks, and preparing for the before, during, and after phases of a school crisis are presented in a simple, clear, and concise manner. Although it is impossible to script every crisis in advance, school and public safety officials, in cooperation with members of the broader school community, can take a number of appropriate steps to reduce the risks of an incident happening and, if necessary, to prepare to manage effectively those incidents that cannot be prevented.

5

Assessing and Managing Threats

All threats must be treated seriously. There must be an understanding that there is no such thing as joking when it comes to threatening harm to others. Educators need to have a protocol in place to evaluate threats and to manage threats in a balanced yet firm and efficient manner.

What do you do when you find a student in possession of a hit list of students and staff to be killed? How do you handle the report that a student threatened to kill a group of other students? What do you do when a teacher reports that a student threatened to kill him or her?

Although there are likely to be some similarities in the general approach to threat assessment, there are some unique factors that make the difference between dealing with school-based, student threats and the kind of threats typically handled by law enforcement officials and private bodyguards responsible for protective details for public officials and foreign dignitaries. The most notable difference is that, in handling school-based threats, educators and law enforcement personnel are dealing with youth behavior and not with the typical adult, terrorist, or other more mature threat sources involved in executive protection. Although there are certainly lessons to be learned from threat assessment outside of the school setting, caution needs to be exercised when considering the various computer software, checklists, and so-called experts attempting to take their expertise from adult settings and apply it directly to school settings without first studying and understanding the differences between adult and juvenile behavior in social settings.

Threat Assessment Protocol

School officials should establish a basic protocol to be followed in assessing and managing student threats. Students need to understand that making threats, even when the student thinks they are not serious, is inappropriate behavior in the school setting. Air travelers cannot joke about guns, bombs, hijacking, or similar issues in an airport, and the same level of seriousness should be applied to the school.

Threat Assessment Questions

No "expert" can accurately predict the exact circumstances surrounding every potential threat that school personnel might encounter. Therefore, educators who rely on profiling checklists of particular circumstances or individual characteristics might not get an accurate read or the best direction for handling every case of student threats. There are, however, some questions that school and public safety officials can use to help them gather as much information as possible to best assess most student threats and to evaluate their best course of action for managing these situations.

Before asking these questions, however, school officials should consider some important lessons learned both from the school violence tragedies of the late 1990s and from the experiences of school safety professionals who have actually prevented violent offenses from occurring elsewhere:

1. There is no particular "look" or appearance that characterizes every individual who might act violently. School officials should therefore exercise caution, and should not evaluate an individual's desire or ability to carry out an act of violence based on appearance. Potential offenders do not necessarily "look crazy" or present an abnormal outward physical appearance. Offenders can, and indeed have, looked like any other "average, ordinary student" in a given school.

2. Officials evaluating threats should focus on *behavior, behavior, behavior!* Educators and public safety officials need to focus on what the threatmakers have done and are doing, not on who they are or appear to be. The threat assessment should be based on the thinking processes and corresponding behaviors of the threatmakers, their position in a continuum of violence or potential violence, and related considerations.

3. A threat alone will not guarantee violence, nor does the absence of a threat guarantee that violence will not occur.

4. Although violent offenders may not make a threat directly to school officials or other potential targets of their violence, they have often told someone that they know, typically other students, about their intended actions. Verbal or other indicators need not be loud and flashy, but they do tend to be present and often detectable by those who are paying close attention.

5. The actions of high-profile violent offenders in schools do not appear to be spontaneous or the result of their acting on impulse, but instead often appear to be planned, thought out, and more organized than a spur-of-the-moment action. In fact, the violent actions in a number of school violence tragedies appear to occur after a progression of deteriorating events

and possibly untreated depression, when offenders have reached a point where they feel that they are at the "end of the road" with no way to turn back and there are no adults or significant others in their life who care about them. When these circumstances exist, or are perceived to exist by the offenders, the resulting violence is often their method for solving such real or perceived problems. Given these conditions, in the end there may be a very thin line between homicide and suicide.

Understanding the mind-set and thinking processes of potentially serious offenders may therefore help educators and public safety officials obtain a more clear and accurate threat assessment.

Keeping the above information in mind, some questions that can guide school officials in assessing any threats coming to their attention include the following:

- What was the motivation of the threat? Are there identifiable reasons why the threat was made?
- What exactly was communicated in the threat? How was it communicated—verbally, or in writing? To whom was the threat communicated?
- In what context did the communication of the threat occur? Was it, for example, in the heat of a fight? In a letter? In a spur-of-the-moment comment?
- What was the intensity of the communicated threat? Was it detailed?
- Does the threatmaker show an unusual interest in violence, weapons, self-abuse, suicide, abuse of animals, or other progressions of violent behavior?
- Has the threatmaker shown an unusual interest in acts of violence committed by others that are similar to those he or she is threatening? Has the person sought out details or studied other similar offenses? Has this unusual action been accompanied by related planning or actions?
- Are there signs of emotional detachment by the threatmaker? If so, to what degree? Is there progressively increasing detachment?
- Has the person making the threat previously engaged in threatening, menacing, harassing, or similar behavior?
- Has the person making the threat previously engaged in planning or committing violent acts?
- If there is a history of violent or threatening behavior, is there a change in the frequency and/or intensity of the incidents?
- Has the person engaged in any specific information-gathering, stalking, or similar activities to learn about the target of his or her threat?
- Does the threatmaker have a plan? If so, how specific is it? Did it include specific steps, maps, or other supportive materials to carry out the threat?

- Does the threatmaker have the ability to carry out the threat?
- Is the threatmaker's overall behavior consistent with his or her threats?
- Does the threatmaker have current or prior undiagnosed and/or untreated mental illness or emotional disturbances, such as depression, delusions, hallucinations, feelings of desperation, feelings of persecution, or similar conditions?
- Have there been any other major stressors or changes in the threatmaker's environment that might affect his or her desire or ability to carry out the threat?
- What action, if any, has been taken in addressing threats previously made by the individual?
- Does the threatmaker have a social support system in school? Outside of school? What is the threatmaker's desire and willingness to seek and accept help?
- Have as many individuals as possible who are familiar with the threatmaker (e.g., teachers, counselors, psychologists, social workers, school support staff, law enforcement, parents, and others) been consulted to obtain a complete picture of the individual? Have others familiar with the threatmaker expressed concern about threats made by the individual?
- Are there any gaps or pieces of missing information that could influence the assessment of the threat?

These and other questions should assist school and public safety officials in focusing on the thinking process and behavior of threatmakers, their position in a continuum of violence or potential violence, and the amount of planning and preparation related to their threat. These questions are not a panacea for evaluating threats, and should not be viewed as a definitive assessment tool. They should, however, illustrate to school officials the importance of establishing some type of guiding protocol questions to help school threat assessment teams process threat incidents. "Flying by the seat of one's pants," rather than having some predetermined questions to ask, will certainly increase the potential for problems.

Threat Management Procedures

Suggested procedures for managing threats once they come to an administrator's attention include, but are not necessarily limited to, the following:

- Treat all threats seriously, and engage a standard rational response protocol for investigating and documenting threats and related actions taken in response to the threats by multidisciplinary school threat assessment teams consisting of administrators, counselors, psychologists, teachers, security/law enforcement personnel, and support staff.

- Interview witnesses to the threat and obtain written witness statements immediately upon notification of the threat.

- Interview the alleged threatmaker, and obtain a written statement from him or her.

- Because one of the more reliable predictors of future behavior is often past behavior, review records of the past disciplinary and criminal behavior of the threatmaker to ascertain if there is a history of such actions.

- Within the legal parameters set on confidentiality, review the psychological history of the threatmaker and confer with counselors and/or psychologists familiar with the individual.

- Assess weapons availability by asking the threatmaker if he or she has access to weapons at home or from other sources.

- Assess weapons availability by asking the threatmaker's parents or guardians if the student has access to weapons and if they are aware of any other threats made by the student.

- Process the various questions and considerations listed in the previous section of this chapter.

- Inspect notebooks, lockers, and book bags for items such as weapons, drawings or essays with violent themes, hit lists, or similar indicators as appropriate. (Reasonable suspicion and related standards for searches will likely need to be taken into consideration.)

- Obtain input from other staff members who know the student, law enforcement officials, and others familiar with the individual and his or her background.

- Notify the police, if appropriate, and do so in a timely manner.

- Secure and maintain custody of related evidence.

- Administer the appropriate disciplinary action.

- Take the necessary steps, if consistent with school policies and procedures, to facilitate formal professional mental health evaluations before the threatmaker returns to school.

- Document the incident.

- Assess the need to provide additional security measures and/or protection to threatened individuals.

- Advise potential victims of administrative, criminal, civil, and other options available to them, such as restraining orders or steps for reporting additional threats or concerns, to prevent or reduce risks of future harm.

- If the threatmaker legally returns to the school setting following disciplinary and/or criminal action, provide an appropriate level of monitoring or follow-up to gauge the individual's behavior.

Recording Threats

Written incident reports of threats and the actions taken to address them should be completed and retained by school and other appropriate personnel. These reports should include, but not necessarily be limited to, the following:

- The name and identification information of the threatmaker, victims, and witnesses
- When and where the threat was made
- How the incident occurred, including conditions and circumstances preceding, surrounding, and following the threat
- Specific language and/or actions associated with the threat
- The names and actions of teachers, support staff, administrators, and other officials involved in assessing and managing the threat
- The steps taken to prevent the threatmaker from carrying out the current threat and/or to prevent future threats
- Steps taken to advise and counsel the victim(s) of the threat

The reports will provide not only documentation of the steps taken by school and other officials to properly manage the threat, but also a written history available for review in assessing related threats that may occur in the future. Issues regarding the retention of these records, security of the records and information contained therein, and legalities of reciprocal information sharing will, of course, also need to be addressed.

Limitations

These steps certainly will not guarantee that threatened harm or additional threats will not occur. However, they do provide school officials with some guidance for treating threats seriously and in a balanced, rational way without over- or underreacting to a threatening situation.

6

A Framework for Reducing Risks

Security, Crisis Preparedness, and Comprehensive Safe Schools Plans

Although no one can guarantee that a school will never experience a tragedy, school officials should be able to identify specific, balanced, and comprehensive steps that they have taken to reduce the risks of such an incident occurring and to prepare to manage a serious incident effectively, should one occur.

The trend of pitting security and crisis preparedness strategies against prevention strategies as an *either/or* option, as discussed in Chapter 1, highlights the tendency Americans have of going from one extreme to the other in their perspectives on how to solve complex problems. Likewise, the inaccurate framing of security and crisis preparedness, equating them with scores of police and tons of equipment in our school hallways, also contributes to a skewed picture of what needs to be done to improve school safety. In order to stand a reasonable chance of making a significant impact on the issue of school safety, a framework based on balance and comprehensives must be acknowledged, accepted, and utilized by those who are working on safe schools issues.

Overcoming Denial

The first and most important step toward reducing security and crisis risks is to acknowledge that the potential for an incident exists in any school district and community in the nation, regardless of location, size, demographics, or other social and economic factors. Although it is logical to believe that this would be a basic premise in the minds of all, denial on individual, school, and community levels is still alive and well. Reasons for denial include

- A perceived need to protect the image and reputation of individuals, schools, and/or communities
- Belief that acknowledgment of the possibility of a security or crisis incident occurring in a school or community equates with a loss of management power, control, and professional or personal security
- Fear that parents and members of the school community will not support levies or other funding drives, and that they may relocate from the community out of fear that schools are unsafe
- Disbelief and distrust of the motives of individuals who publicly persist in putting safe schools on the agenda (i.e., the belief that these individuals are grandstanding, have personal or professional aspirations behind their efforts, or that they are alarmists)
- The sincere belief that "It can't happen here" or that "It won't happen in *my* school or *my* community"

The hazards of continued denial are many, and include the following:

- Denial in the short term leading to higher losses in the long term
- Increased, not decreased, safety risks
- Promotion of the wrong message to offenders, leading them to believe that their behavior is acceptable and tolerated
- Reductions in the productivity of individuals on the front lines who perceive—many times appropriately so—a lack of support from those who are higher up and in denial
- Denial communicating that school officials are not concerned about safety and that they are not responsive to the needs and desires of members of the school community
- A reduction of the knowledge base on a problem, because, due to denial, the problems are not fully identified, researched, or funded for solutions
- An adverse impact on an organization's or community's economic base because the failure to acknowledge and act on a problem or concern is interpreted as neglect or a cover-up (this perception generates a lack of trust in and support for the organization and its leaders, which can lead to a lack of support for funding drives or relocation from the community)

In the end, the costs of denial are far greater than the benefits. Once everyone acknowledges a problem or the potential for a problem, they can then move on in their efforts to prevent and manage the problem.

Financial Obstacles

I have listened to school board members, superintendents, and other educational administrators dismiss security and crisis preparedness suggestions by simply claiming, "Whatever it is, it costs too much. It is either security or textbooks and, since we're a school district, education is our top priority and the money must go directly to learning." There are several inherent problems with this line of thinking.

First and foremost, the first priority must be school safety. Common sense (something often lacking in policy-making and legislative decisions) dictates that children and teachers who are preoccupied with their safety will not have their maximum attention focused on the educational process. In other words, for true education to occur, school officials must first create a safe and secure environment in which to deliver the educational programs.

A second problem with this line of thinking is that security and crisis preparedness are being automatically framed as such high-ticket items as manpower or equipment. Ironically, in our assessments of school security for districts nationwide, we typically find that these items are often last on the list, if they even make it at all, in terms of safety needs. Typically, a lack of training and awareness, combined with inadequately enforced security policies and procedures, top the list of safety needs in most schools.

Realistically, there are some areas for improvement that simply require dollars, especially those associated with physical security improvements. There simply is no way to duck and dodge the need to pay for some risk reduction measures, although incorporating such needs into capital improvement budgets and long-term strategic plans may be one appropriate step toward doing what is right to reduce risks and still managing the financial end of school operations. To expect to create schools without some costs is unrealistic and impractical.

Perhaps the best way to look at the financial aspect of implementing safe school measures is to look not at the cost of doing *something*, but instead at the cost of doing *nothing*. By taking no steps to reduce school safety risks, educators face the following potential costs:

- Increased risks for successful legal action against a school district and/or its individual employees due to inadequate security, and increased legal costs associated with defending unsuccessful lawsuits or paying off settlements for cases that do not go to trial

- Increased insurance claims against the school district for injuries and losses associated with violence, property damage, and other criminal activity

- Potentially massive unplanned costs associated with a recovery from a crisis or disaster, such as increased manpower and overtime costs, major repairs to the physical facility, and increased legal and public relations support services

- An inability to recruit and retain quality staff due to real or perceived unsafe workplace conditions

- An inability to improve test scores and other areas of student achievement due to a decreased focus on academics stemming from an increased focus on safety

In the end, the costs of doing nothing certainly outweigh the costs of taking reasonable, practical, and cost-effective measures to reduce school safety risks.

From a PR Nightmare to a PR Tool

School safety has experienced a complete turnaround in terms of public relations. In the past, many educators felt that by publicly addressing school safety and crisis preparedness, they were setting themselves up for a public relations nightmare by simply talking about the subject. Today, there has been a complete turnaround, to the point that, in a number of cities after the Columbine tragedy, educators were literally holding press conferences to announce the steps they were taking to improve school safety.

Although some school officials chose to misuse the issue of school safety not only for public relations, but also for political and personal gain, the use of the issue to gain some positive public relations by a school district is not necessarily a bad thing as long as the district is truly doing what it says it is doing. Public relations has, unfortunately, become a negative phrase, when in reality it should simply mean communicating the good behavior of school district officials in an effective manner. As long as the school officials are sincere and are actually doing something in addition to talking about doing it, there is nothing wrong with school safety being a positive public relations tool.

Higher-Risk Threats

Some types of individuals, situations, times, and places encountered by school officials are, by their nature, higher risk than others in terms of safety threats. These include

- Athletic events, especially, but not only, when there are a large number of observers or when the games are between rivals
- Dances and similar social events where there are a large number of individuals gathered together and engaging in increased social activities
- Locations within and around the school where there is a high level of student movement but little responsible adult supervision, such as restrooms, isolated hallways, stairwells, cafeterias, and bus drop-off and pick-up points
- At school opening, during class change times, and at dismissal
- Irate parents or guardians, especially when they have ongoing encounters with school officials that they perceive to be negative or adversarial
- Disgruntled employees who cannot resolve their conflicts through formal and legitimate mechanisms

It is logical to believe that, because we know what types of situations pose a higher risk, we should be able to take more risk reduction measures to counter them. Unfortunately, this is not always the case.

Risk Reduction Framework

The Security and Crisis Preparedness Components

Steps should be taken in at least four basic risk reduction categories associated with school security and crisis preparedness. These include

1. Firm, fair, and consistent enforcement of safety-related policies and procedures, along with adequate and effective levels of adult supervision

2. Training, as appropriate, on security and crisis threat trends and strategies for *all* school personnel, including support staff, such as secretaries, custodians, and bus drivers, as well as other key members of the school community

3. Professional school security assessments conducted by qualified professionals, such as in-house school security specialists, school resource officers, or qualified outside school security consultants, and the implementation of appropriate recommendations stemming from such an assessment

4. Creation, testing, updating, and revising crisis preparedness guidelines for natural disasters and crises stemming from man- made acts of crime and violence

These four broad categories, and the many specific measures that are a part of the respective processes or process outcomes, can contribute toward reducing security and crisis-related risks.

A Comprehensive Safe Schools Framework

Security and crisis preparedness represent only two pieces of a comprehensive safe schools framework. A balanced and comprehensive safe schools framework includes these parts as the first line of defense and prevention, but also will include them as a part of an overall plan that includes, but is not necessarily limited to,

- Proactive security measures
- Crisis preparedness planning
- Firm, fair, and consistent discipline
- Effective prevention and intervention programs
- Mental health support services
- A school climate stressing respect, acceptance of diversity, belonging, trust, pride, ownership, involvement, peaceful resolution of conflicts, and related characteristics

- Strong and challenging academic programs supplemented by diverse extracurricular activities
- Parental and community involvement, support, and networking

All of these components should receive equal attention in developing a safe schools plan. To focus too strongly on only one or a handful, but not all, will reduce the likelihood of having an effective, comprehensive strategy for reducing safety risks.

What Works?

General Approaches

From a practical, frontline perspective, I have found that the following approaches contribute significantly to safe schools:

- Order, structure, and firm, fair, and consistent discipline
- A genuine balance between prevention, intervention, security, and crisis preparedness strategies
- Individual assessment and intervention with children experiencing academic and behavioral problems
- Sincere relationships between students and staff, and staff and the broader school community (e.g., with parents, social services, law enforcement, support personnel, etc.)
- Information sharing, within legal boundaries and not in violation of legitimate confidentiality parameters, between schools and law enforcement, criminal justice officials, social service representatives, parents, and relevant other youth service providers
- Youth service providers, parents, and others who are consistently alert, informed, and proactive in addressing youth and violence prevention issues
- Simple, apolitical, and youth-focused action

Ironically, most of these items require more time than they do money. Either way, we cannot continue to ask ourselves why our efforts at preventing school and youth violence are not working when we are not willing to invest fully both our time and money into doing so.

Security and Crisis Preparedness Approaches

The hot-button issues tend to change quickly in any field, but the focus on school security and crisis preparedness will likely be with us for a long time to come. Several strategies of particular interest following the school shootings are listed below:

School Security Assessments. Although my first book, *Practical School Security* (Trump, 1998), covers the subject of school security assessments in more detail, it is directly related to the focus of this book in that school assessments have become increasingly popular since the school shootings of the late 1990s. A professional assessment of safety issues will identify and reinforce positive risk reduction measures already in place, as well as make recommendations for improvements. Assessments help to keep balance without overreaction or denial, while serving as a strategic plan to reduce risks and to improve school safety.

School security assessments should not, however, be presented as

- A guarantee that a crisis will never occur
- An attack on individuals or their management ability
- Single-strategy focused, such as curriculum-only or equipment-only
- Product-driven instead of process-driven
- Generic, canned, or rhetorical one-size-fits-all reports
- A panacea or final cure for all school safety concerns

School security and crisis preparedness strategies are not an event, but rather a part of a process. These strategies must be present at all times, and persons involved in the safe schools process must be thinking about them as much at times when there is no crisis as they do immediately following a high-profile crisis.

Some of the best practices in conducting school security assessments include

- Distinguishing safety, which is freedom from accidental injuries, from the concept of security, which is freedom from intentional harm or loss
- Avoiding relying solely on checklists for assessing school security
- Remembering not to compare excessively the security issues of one school or district with another
- Accounting for unique issues and needs of individual schools and districts
- Reviewing risk reduction measures taken by other schools or districts, but tailoring such measures to individual schools or districts instead of simply copying the plans and procedures of someone else
- Avoiding the use of security equipment vendors, nonsecurity professionals, and security specialists with no K-12 school security experience to conduct school security assessments

School officials also need to recognize that there are multiple levels of assessment with accompanying pros and cons:

1. There is *no assessment* at all, which requires no immediate costs but increases risks for security problems and higher liability in the long term.

2. There is *self-assessment*, which typically has low costs except for time investments, but may lack specialized knowledge in security and crisis areas and also has a higher risk of a flawed process, especially considering the potential for political and personal influences in self-assessments.

3. There is *assessment by other governmental agencies*, which may have no cost or low costs and may offer more area-specific knowledge, but may also afford no control over the quality or experience of the assessors and could involve other bureaucratic issues.

4. There is also *assessment by outside specialists*, which offers an independent and specialized expertise working for the school district, but one which typically costs more than the other options.

Unfortunately, following the shootings of the late 1990s, an explosion of overnight experts and charlatans have identified themselves as school security "experts" in order to offer assessment and other services to school officials. These individuals have included everyone from former law enforcement agents to former educators. School leaders should exercise caution in selecting individuals to conduct school security assessments to avoid consultants who increase risks for additional public embarrassment and liability to the schools and whose recommendations might increase safety risks.

School Resource Officers and Security Staffing. Although the placement of law enforcement officers, typically known as school resource officers (SROs), in schools has grown tremendously over the past decade, the move to do so appears to have increased dramatically following the school shootings of the late 1990s. Various forms of security staffing are being used across the country, and no single staffing method is the only and absolute approach for all schools, as each has its own set of pros and cons. In fact, it is not uncommon to use a combination of approaches, such as SROs and school security officials working side-by-side in a school.

SROs are typically city or county law enforcement officers assigned by their departments to work in the schools within their jurisdiction. The schools benefit by having trained, certified peace officers available to focus on law enforcement, counseling, and education programs related to the law and law enforcement. Funding, personnel selection, supervision, and other operational logistics should be addressed in the early stages of an SRO program.

The SRO model can be a win-win arrangement for schools, law enforcement agencies, and the community when selection, supervision, financial details, and other logistics are worked out on the front end of a program. An SRO program can provide quality, cost-effective service for schools and police departments alike. It also typically improves school crime reporting procedures and the sharing of information on school and community juvenile crime activity between the district and the police.

School-based policing, like the overall school security and crisis preparedness profession, must be viewed as a distinguished, professional discipline. Contrary to the perception that SRO programs simply mean having another "warm body with a gun" in the school hallway, an appropriately selected, trained, and qualified SRO performs many more tasks associated with prevention than with arrest and prosecution in schools. A successful SRO program depends on its design from the outset, and school and public safety officials would be wise to consult with the nation's leading organization on school-based policing, the National Association of School Resource Officers (NASRO), to learn how to operate such a program. (See NASRO's website at *www.nasro.org.*)

Other forms of school security staffing may exist and be quite appropriate as well. A number of schools nationwide have their own in-house school security personnel whose titles often vary and may include *school security officer, school safety officer,* or *campus supervisor*. Some states also allow school police departments to have sworn, certified peace officers work exclusively for the school district performing police and safety functions.

School Security Equipment and Technology. Unfortunately, a number of school districts have created a false sense of security in response to recent high-profile school violence tragedies by moving quickly to install equipment and other physical and tangible measures, often for the sake of having something concrete to show students, staff, parents, the media, and the overall school community as evidence that they have worked on improving school safety. Educators need to ensure that they do not use equipment and technology in school safety programs as a panacea for solving safety concerns.

On the other hand, when effectively utilized and employed under the appropriate circumstances, equipment can contribute to reducing school safety risks. Rather than simply having equipment for the sake of having equipment, however, school officials should focus on answering the following questions:

- What specific security threats are we attempting to address?
- How will the equipment help address these threats?
- If we are able to purchase the equipment, who will use it, how will it be used, and how will it be maintained and repaired?

Educators who can answer these questions in detail will likely be in a much better position to receive the maximum benefits from the use of school security equipment and technology.

School Design and Architecture. The design of a school and its surrounding campus can play a significant role in preventing crime and facilitating school safety measures. School officials involved in designing new school facilities or remodeling existing school sites should consider doing the following:

- Insist on being involved in the design process and work with architects and construction personnel in the early stages to provide input on how the school design can help improve supervision and safety.
- Consider carefully the placement of common areas, sites used extensively for after-hours events (e.g., gyms, auditoriums, cafeterias, and libraries), and other key locations to help control access and limit use requiring movement or open access to all areas of the school in the evening.
- Review parking lot placement, size, and related factors to best facilitate safe movement and supervision.
- Consider the importance of line of sight in hallways and areas requiring supervision.
- Take into consideration opportunities for natural surveillance and supervision by placing areas of greater activity or higher risk in areas where there will be higher levels of adult supervision.
- Involve school security officials, SROs, and/or outside school safety specialists in the planning and design of new or remodeled facilities. Their perspectives may provide very different, but valuable, insights.

It is much easier to put crime prevention measures into the initial designs of a school and its surrounding campus than it is to attempt to retrofit security measures after a structure is already in place.

Incident Reporting and Analysis. The only thing more important than collecting data on school crimes is the analysis of the data collected. School districts should develop standard incident report forms to record the *Who, What, When, Where, Why,* and *How* of all serious disciplinary and criminal incidents occurring on school grounds or in situations under school jurisdiction. Some schools have even created pin maps and computerized tracking systems that chart disciplinary and criminal incidents by classroom, hallway, and other areas of the building to identify patterns and ongoing problem areas. The cumulative data collected from these incidents should be analyzed on a regular and ongoing basis to identify trends and preventive action to be taken to reduce future occurrences.

Crisis Simulations, Exercises, and Scenarios. Following the Columbine incident in April 1999, a number of schools dramatically expanded their crisis preparedness planning. This included not only forming crisis teams and developing written guidelines, but also conducting tabletop exercise discussions or actual full-scale mock crisis simulation exercises. Properly done, these efforts can help effectively prepare school, public safety, and other interested parties to prevent and, if necessary, better manage a crisis.

Additional thoughts on crisis preparedness will be discussed in the following chapter.

III

Crisis Preparedness and Management

Unfortunately, no matter how much school and public safety officials work to prevent a crisis or serious security incident, such a tragedy may still occur. In addition to reducing risks in an effort to prevent such occurrences, individuals responsible for school safety should be prepared to manage effectively and efficiently those incidents that cannot be prevented.

Chapter 7 lays out the nuts and bolts of the crisis planning process, crisis guideline document contents and formats, and many steps that can be taken to prepare for effectively managing a school crisis. Chapter 8 then discusses the various roles, responsibilities, and actions crisis team members should consider when planning their guidelines for response. Chapter 9 concludes this section with a look at the post-crisis crisis of dealing with communications, media, counseling, healing, litigation, and financial issues.

7

Crisis Preparedness Guidelines
Process, Product, and Preparation Issues

No person can perfectly script every possible crisis, but having no guidelines at all in today's education world could legitimately be considered as negligence. The key rests somewhere between doing nothing and "paralysis by analysis."

Where do we start? Where do we stop? These are two of the most commonly asked questions about the crisis planning process in our crisis preparedness workshops for school personnel. Giving recommendations for where to start is not too difficult depending on where the people asking the question actually are in the process. Knowing when enough is enough, however, is the more difficult task.

This chapter offers a starting point to beginners and a refresher to the veteran crisis planner. In both cases, there are a number of questions that crisis planners will need to ask when developing their guidelines. No book or "expert" can answer all of these questions without being familiar with the individual school or school district.

Normalization Nonsense

A number of academicians, educators, and others have claimed that the presence of security and related crisis preparedness measures normalize violence, imply that violence is expected, or actually increase the level of fear by sending the message that kids are vulnerable to violence due to their presence. Although this might sound logical in theory, it lacks practicality and common sense when used to justify not having reasonable security and crisis preparedness measures in and around our schools.

Using this same line of thought, it could then be considered logical and acceptable to

- Stop conducting fire drills because they increase the fear that a fire may occur
- Eliminate law enforcement personnel from our society because their presence might send a message that violence is to be expected
- Remove security personnel, metal detectors, and X-ray machines from airports so that we do not communicate our fear and distrust to terrorists and bombers
- Leave the doors and windows to our homes open when we are not present so that we do not communicate to burglars that we expect someone might break into our homes, steal our valuables, and/or harm us upon our return

These thoughts are, of course, as ludicrous as the suggestion that school security and crisis preparedness measures, police presence and collaboration with schools, and related measures contribute to school violence.

Unfortunately, this type of Ivory Tower theory has received an excessive amount of coverage in the media, has made undue input into legislative considerations, and has spurred overall debate on the school safety issue. This problem is further exacerbated by the absence of research on school security and crisis preparedness measures (see Chapter 11). One can only assume that individuals who subscribe to this type of thinking, and who in turn advocate not having professional security and crisis preparedness programs, must have experienced unprofessional security programs, must never have been victims of crime, or are so far removed from reality that their ability to influence school or public policy should be closely scrutinized.

A reasonable number of security and crisis preparedness measures are necessary to reduce the risks posed by security threats and to minimize losses that may occur in managing crises. Testing crisis guidelines is necessary to ensure that the guidelines do not just look good on paper, but that they also work. Security guidelines and measures also reflect reality, making everyone aware of what needs to be done in the event of a crisis situation.

School officials should, however, consciously balance the need to reduce risks and prepare for crises with the need to avoid creating fear or panic. The most effective way to do so is for school officials to communicate clearly the rationale for conducting such exercises to students, staff, and parents, and to plan actual exercises that are carefully thought out from both an operational and a legal perspective. When properly informed, these individuals typically understand why the activities are taking place and, more important, appreciate that school and safety officials are taking steps to reduce risks and to prepare for successfully managing a crisis incident, should one occur.

Lockdown drills, for example, have falsely been equated to prison lockdowns by some individuals. Although lockdown procedures have grown tremendously as a result of the attention to high-profile school shootings, there are a number of reasons why a school official may want to be able to have students and staff quickly cleared from the hallways and relocated to more secure areas of the school, including a number of reasons that have nothing to do with crimes. For example, a loose hostile animal biting children in the school's hallway might be a very good reason for calling a lockdown throughout the school.

The bottom line on both sides of this issue is common sense. Schools should not resemble prisons, nor should students be treated like prisoners. The adults running schools, however, also have a responsibility to take reasonable steps to protect students and staff, and to prepare to manage effectively those security violations and crisis incidents that may not be preventable.

The Process

The crisis preparedness planning process should include at least ten basic steps:

1. Appoint a district-level crisis team and building-level crisis team.

2. Determine realistic goals and objectives for the crisis teams.

3. Research guidelines and resources for developing crisis guidelines that are in place in other schools.

4. Review and, if necessary, modify existing school policies, and recommend new policies, if appropriate.

5. Identify resources within the individual school, at the district level, and within the community, and consider the following questions:

   - What is the source and level of response to be anticipated from local emergency service personnel, such as police, fire, and medical? What type of equipment and resources will these agencies have available? Will a serious incident, such as a bomb threat or suspicious device, hazardous material exposure, or other crisis, require emergency service expertise from outside of the regular departments, and, if so, how long do we wait and what should we do (or not do) while waiting?

   - If counselors, psychologists, and other mental health professionals are needed, can they be drawn from other schools within the district, and, if so, how? Will they need to come from other districts or community agencies? If yes, what is the mobilization process, and is it documented?

   - What communications capabilities exist or do not exist? In addition to telephones, is there an adequate number of two-way radio units and who has them? Do they function in all, or just some, areas of the school and surrounding campus? Are multiagency communications systems compatible with one another? What are the limitations of the phone communications system in the general school area and/or elsewhere? What, if any, alternative communications plans exist? How can technology be effectively utilized to manage communications concerns?

6. Conduct, or have a qualified professional conduct, a school security assessment, and review and reevaluate plans at least annually.

7. Develop crisis guidelines in a two-directional manner to ensure that guidelines are not simply issued in a top-down fashion without the input and ownership of the building staff and that individual building teams are addressing common issues.

8. Have the final draft versions of the crisis guidelines reviewed by key stakeholders in the process within and outside of the district, including emergency service providers and school attorneys.

9. Test and revise the guidelines, and train all staff on them.

10. Integrate the crisis preparedness guidelines into the broader, more comprehensive school safety plan, and make this plan an ongoing process within the school community.

Staying focused and keeping the steps in the process to a manageable number will help school officials develop worthwhile guidelines without falling into paralysis by analysis.

Crisis Team Levels and Composition

District-level crisis teams should coordinate central office support with the building crisis team staff, and crisis teams at the building level should focus on directly managing students, staff, parents, and others with whom they are the most familiar. Certainly the work of the two teams will overlap, but building-level school staff are typically more familiar with the individuals directly affected by the crisis incident, as well as with the physical school plant itself; they will, therefore, be better positioned to interact effectively with those directly involved in the crisis. District-level staff typically are in a better position quickly to mobilize additional resources, such as transportation, counselors and personnel from other district schools, community-based resources, media liaison officials, and other support services to assist building-level crisis officials in restoring order and crisis recovery efforts.

Crisis team members at the building level should include

- The principal, assistant principals, and/or deans
- School resource officers and security personnel or campus supervisors
- Counselors, social workers, and psychologists
- Custodians

- Secretaries
- School nurses
- The cafeteria manager
- Key teachers
- A parent representative
- A student representative
- Others identified by crisis team members as playing key roles in crisis management

District level crisis team members should include

- A representative of the school board
- The superintendent and assistant superintendent(s)
- The district safety and security supervisor
- The business manager
- The transportation supervisor
- A media spokesperson
- Maintenance and/or physical plant supervisors
- Counseling and psychological support service supervisors
- The supervisor of discipline and related support services
- The school attorney and other key district-level support personnel who would provide critical support to schools during a crisis

Although both teams should interact with emergency service personnel and other key agencies and individuals in the broader community, the district-level crisis team should take a lead in formulating formal and informal relationships with those community members outside of the school district who would play an important role in crisis prevention and management. Such organizations might include

- The police
- The fire department
- Emergency medical services
- Hazardous materials crews
- Public works agencies
- Regional or state emergency management agencies
- Mental health and social service agencies
- Criminal justice professionals (e.g., court, probation, and parole officers)
- The clergy
- The media
- Elected officials
- Members of the business community
- Other community leaders

The key is for district crisis team members to take the lead in formalizing relationships with individuals and agencies in the larger community who will interact with school officials in a crisis situation.

Team Member Characteristics

Community and school district size, available resources, and individual personalities will all play a role in determining the characteristics of your crisis team membership. Desired characteristics of crisis team members include the following:

- Strong verbal and written communication abilities
- The ability to remain calm, confident, deliberate, and focused
- The ability and authority to make logical decisions under stress
- A willingness and ability to take directions, to work as a team, and also to work independently when necessary
- Flexibility, adaptability, and the ability to "go with the flow"
- Being task oriented, but with ability to empathize and be people oriented as well
- Firmness, fairness, and consistency in dealing with others

Crisis team leaders should be familiar with the team members, their strengths and weaknesses, and the best possible match between members and team roles whenever possible.

The Product: Crisis Guideline Documents

Once the parameters of the crisis preparedness process have been identified and the crisis team members have been selected, the next questions tend to be, "What should the final 'product' of the process include?" and "How should it look when it is completed?"

Begin With a Board Policy

School board leaders should establish a policy requiring that their districts establish crisis guidelines for themselves and their individual buildings. The policy should include

- A position statement demonstrating that the need to be proactive on safety and crisis preparedness issues is recognized by school leaders
- A direction to district administrators to implement a comprehensive school safety plan that includes security and crisis preparedness, prevention and intervention, mental health, firm and fair discipline, school climate, and other related school safety components

School board members should research the policies of neighboring districts and those on file with their state and national professional associations when developing the parameters of their own policy. Furthermore, all policies should be reviewed by legal counsel before implementation.

Plagiarism Versus "Modified Borrowing"

Educators are notorious for "borrowing" materials and ideas from other school districts on a variety of matters. Providing that appropriate credit is given and that plagiarism does not occur, there is nothing wrong with one school adapting the lessons learned from other schools to their particular school or district. The key, however, is to have the borrowed information or materials *modified and adapted* to the school or district doing the borrowing.

The growing trend toward having crisis guidelines in school districts has, unfortunately, led some school officials simply to take the crisis documents from one district, change the names on the document, and then disseminate it as their own crisis document. This effort to have a product simply for the sake of having a product is exceptionally dangerous because it has not been adapted to fit the borrowing school or district and because it lacks ownership by that group's members. It also represents a potentially increased liability to borrowing school officials should they be legally challenged as to the source of their plan, how it was developed, and related issues.

Plans or Guidelines? A Lesson Plan for Crises

Many educators struggle to understand exactly what a crisis plan or guideline actually is meant to be. The best way for educators to conceptualize crisis guidelines is to view them as they do their classroom lesson plans.

The purpose of a lesson plan is to provide some guidance and direction for the teacher to follow in managing the instructional session. Lesson plans typically identify goals and objectives, and then build a guiding framework for the teacher to follow in getting to the desired end result of the lesson. Most experienced teachers use lesson plans as guides rather than as rigid scripts to be followed without flexibility or adaptation. In short, although they are called *plans*, they are really *guidelines* used to move progressively through a process to reach a desired outcome. (Perhaps the name should be changed to *lesson guidelines?*)

Although possibly a minor, trivial difference in the eyes of some, a closer look at the term *guidelines* suggests something different from plans. Although the term *plan* suggests a very concrete, rigid, and sequential step-by-step process, guidelines are

- Structured, yet flexible
- Guiding, but less "scripted"
- Adaptable to allow effective management of the changing and unpredictable flow of a crisis

Real-life crisis situations cannot be scripted down to the last detail, and, for crisis guidelines to be effective, they must allow crisis responders to exercise some level of adaptability, flexibility, and movement as the crisis unfolds, just as a teacher does with lesson plans.

This distinction of conceptualization and verbiage is not only important in crisis preparedness process and final product, but it could also very well play a role in litigation if a district is challenged on its crisis preparedness and response. It would seem much more reasonable to indicate that the end product produced by crisis teams should be viewed as guidelines, with room for adaptability and flexibility, rather than as rigid procedural plans that must be followed to the letter regardless of the circumstances.

The Product Document Format

The last thing most people will do in the middle of a crisis is read a 300-page crisis manual to tell them what to do in a crisis! Yet, ironically, we have seen a number of crisis guideline documents that are inches (if not more than a foot) thick.

Although a more detailed manual might be appropriate for top central office administrators and perhaps the building principal's reference library, documents for building administrators, teachers, and support staff should be simple, accessible, clear, and direct. A multilayered flip-chart with bulleted steps or checklists seems to be the most practical format for use by those on the front lines of the crisis. The importance of keeping it simple, direct, and accessible to those who need it cannot be overstated.

Defining a School Crisis

As I have been advised by a number of superintendents and board members, what may be a crisis for one person might not necessarily be a crisis to another in day-to-day operations. In a crisis, however, it is important for everyone to be on the same page in terms of defining what is and is not a crisis. A common definition should therefore be established by the crisis team.

A school crisis may be defined as

> an incident occurring at a location under school control or in the community that negatively affects a large number of students, staff, and/or other members of the school community.

This is only one example, however, and whether a definition is appropriate ultimately depends on whether or not it is agreed upon and recognized as such by crisis team members and those who are being served by the crisis guidelines (i.e., students, staff, etc.).

Establishing Crisis Criteria

To help make any crisis definition operational, school officials may wish to elaborate on the definition by establishing criteria that must be present for an incident to be considered a crisis. These might include incidents that

- Are life-threatening
- Pose a threat to the health, safety, and welfare of students, staff, and community

- Create, or have the potential to create, a severe disruption to or interruption of the education process or normal school operations
- Might not appear to be a crisis, but that are judged, based on past experiences or circumstances unique to the school or community, to have a potential to create crisis conditions

A general understanding of the crisis definition and its criteria is critical to ensuring a timely response. It is also very wise to work with public safety officials on the definition as well so that all players within the community are on the same page from the onset of crisis preparedness planning.

Crisis Levels

Different types of crisis situations warrant different levels of response. Crisis team members may wish to distinguish the differences among types of crisis situations by their potential severity and corresponding responses. For example, school officials could create a three-tiered system:

1. *Level One:* Crisis situations that pose a minor disruption to school operations or pose a lower-level threat to student and staff safety, but are outside of daily disciplinary issues and require prompt attention. Level One situations typically would be handled by officials within the school.

2. *Level Two:* Crisis situations that pose a moderate disruption to school operations or pose a moderate threat to student and staff safety. Level Two situations would require limited assistance from outside of the school.

3. *Level Three:* Crisis situations that pose a serious disruption to school operations or pose a serious threat to student and staff safety. Level Three situations would require a large amount of support from elsewhere within the school district and from the outside community.

These three levels are very generic examples. Crisis team members interested in applying a multilevel system for classifying crisis situations should spend some time discussing the various types of "What if?" situations and the types of responses to these situations when defining the various crisis levels for their guidelines.

Minimum Crisis Guideline Components

How far is far enough in terms of what to include in crisis documents? How do you avoid a 300-page crisis document when there are so many possibilities that could be included in the guidelines? These are typically the first questions on the minds of most school administrators and crisis team members who take on the task of developing a crisis guideline document.

Minimum Four Components. A number of crisis guidelines that I have reviewed over the years have focused either on the mental health crisis perspective (e.g., on providing counselors and psychologists dealing with deaths, suicide threats, etc.) or on the criminal perspective (e.g., on dealing with shootings, hostage situations, etc.). Others have focused largely on dealing with the media, or have listed more background information on policies, procedures, or preventive programs as their crisis guidelines. Fewer schools have had a balanced and comprehensive, yet clear and concise, guideline document that covers crisis response procedures clearly without adding up to an extremely large end product.

First, school officials should distinguish their crisis response guidelines from documents listing their policies, procedures, and prevention and intervention programs. These areas are all important components of the overall school safety plan, but they are not something that will need to be read by people on the front lines in the middle of the crisis incident.

Crisis guideline documents should include the following four basic sections and the various subcategories that may develop under each:

1. A bullet-style list of guidelines for "What if?" situations (see later sections in this chapter), along with evacuation and lockdown guidelines, staging area information, and related preparation materials

2. A description of the expected roles and responsibilities for specific staff positions and/or individuals on the crisis team, as well as those not on the team but being affected by the crisis

3. Communications guidelines (internal and external) and related resource listings, such as individual names, agencies, phone numbers, and other contact information

4. Counseling, healing, and related mental health support guidelines

It is difficult to keep the amount of information under each of these sections as focused and concise as possible, but these categories should provide crisis team members with some reasonable parameters for feeling comfortable that they have covered the critical areas needed in the crisis guidelines without overkill.

"What If?" Situations. Addressing "What if?" situations simply means playing out a particular scenario or type of crisis incident: What if there is a bus accident and we have a large number of students injured? What if there is a shooting in the cafeteria? What if we have a hostage situation? What if we are dealing with adults instead of juveniles?

By walking through a tabletop discussion of various types of "What if?" situations and creating bullet-style lists of things that would need to be done, crisis team members can develop some practical, realistic steps to be included in their crisis guidelines. This need not be an extremely long process; in fact, I demonstrate how easily and effectively this can be done in our crisis workshops by tossing out a preestablished "What if?" scenario to crisis team members and having them report their steps back to the larger group in less than 10 minutes. Participants are often amazed at how much they were able to list in such a short time, illustrating the point that although the crisis preparedness process requires more time and effort than it does money and equipment, a rather comprehensive list of things to do can be developed in a relatively short period of time.

There are two keys to success in this process, however:

1. Have the right players at the table so that all of the different perspectives are represented and have input. The teacher's perspective on what will need to be done is typically different from that of the principal, which is also different from the secretary's perspective or the superintendent's, and so on.

2. Use common sense to know when to draw the line in the "What if?" process. I have watched people play out "What if?" scenarios to the extreme! For example, in one scenario involving a bomb threat evacuation, team members appropriately played out the scenario to ensure that they moved children not only out of the building where a suspicious device had been found, but also away from cars in the parking lot to an adjacent open school field in case additional bomb devices had been planted in the cars. This demonstrated a good level of thinking things out, but then the group got carried away with other "What if?" possibilities: What if there are snipers on the hills around the schools? What if somebody does a drive-by shooting?

Crisis team members need to be flexible, creative, and insightful enough to carry their thinking out beyond the surface of a situation. But they also need to apply common sense and, most important, to recognize the importance of limiting how far they carry out the process, because the realm of possible scenarios is endless. Those who fail to draw the line are, unfortunately, the people who tend to be pulling out their hair in this process.

There are some general suggestions that apply to almost all crisis situations. These should be common to most "What if?" situations and, to avoid unnecessary duplication, could be provided in crisis guideline documents under one general heading instead of being repeated in the bulleted list for every type of incident. They include the following:

- Remain as calm and composed as possible.
- Focus on protecting lives and assisting the injured as opposed to protecting school property or personal belongings.
- Give clear, short, specific, and direct verbal commands, and, if appropriate, reinforce them with simple and understandable hand commands when directing students and others in a crisis.
- Know how to report situations; that is, to provide information on *where, what, who, when,* and *how* when reporting concerns to or seeking assistance from outside agencies or internally to other school officials.
- Once an incident is over and your immediate recovery needs have been met, be sure to document your observations and actions in a timely and thorough manner.

Noncriminal "What If?" Situations. School officials have generally done a good job in preparing for noncriminal "What if?" situations, such as fires, weather and natural disasters, or unanticipated deaths of students or staff. In developing school crisis guidelines, the noncriminal "What if?" situations covered should include

- Accidents with a large number of injuries, such as a school bus accident, airplane crash, or other mass catastrophe
- Death, serious illness, or other medical situations involving students or staff
- Environmental issues, such as hazardous materials release, chemical spills, or toxic waste
- Fire or explosions (such as a boiler explosion)
- Utility-related situations, such as a gas leak, or a power or water outage
- Student or adult demonstrations or protests (note, however, that these could translate into criminal situations)
- Weather-related situations, such as a tornado, a severe storm, floods, hurricanes, earthquakes, or other area-specific possibilities

Criminal "What If?" Situations. Schools have historically not included a substantial number of situations in their crisis guidelines related to violence or criminal activity. Situations that should be included in this section include

- Abductions, such as kidnapping and abductions of children by a noncustodial parent
- Altercations or riots, including large-scale fights, racially motivated conflicts, and gang-related disruptions
- Bomb threats and suspicious devices
- A drug overdose by multiple individuals
- Gunfire in the school or on school grounds
- Hostage situations
- Terroristic threats, such as Anthrax scares
- Trespassers, suspicious persons, or other intruders
- Weapons possession, threats, and use
- Violations of other laws and ordinances

Unique conditions in individual schools and communities may very well warrant the expansion of both the noncriminal and criminal "What if?" categories. These lists are included here as a starting point, not as a panacea.

Going through "What if?" situations as a part of crisis preparedness planning, coupled with adequate in-service training, can help educators reduce their fear of the unknown and prepare to better manage incidents of crime and violence for which they otherwise would not have received training. For example, in a hostage situation, it is generally advisable to remain calm and avoid being agitated; to be patient and allow time to pass without losing confidence in the police negotiators; to keep distance from the hostage-taker and avoid aggressive or threatening body movements; and consciously to remember that, as a hostage, educators are no longer in control. Knowing a few basic tips and what to expect from law enforcement response units in a hostage situation can prevent educators from unintentionally escalating, instead of de-escalating, a life-threatening situation.

Evacuations and Lockdown Procedures

Depending on the nature of the crisis, school officials may have to evacuate the building, lockdown the building, or do both simultaneously. For example, evacuations may be necessary in a fire situation, bomb threat, or location of a suspicious device, whereas a lockdown may be needed during situations with intruders, hostages, gunfire, or similar circumstances. Evacuations and lockdowns may need to occur at the same time if a crisis situation requires students and staff in one area of the school to remain there while others located elsewhere are ordered to exit the building.

Evacuations and Alternative Sites. Schools have generally done good jobs with evacuations for fire drills, and, depending on the situation, the same general procedure may be appropriate for other situations. In some cases, however, it may not be adequate. For example, evacuation to a parking lot area works fine in a fire drill, but in a bomb scare school officials may prefer to locate students in an adjacent open field so that they are away from vehicles in the event that someone placed a bomb in one or more of the cars.

An alternative evacuation site should be established for every school district building. In ideal situations, these sites would be places near the school, such as a church, community center, business facility, or other adequately sized location to which students and staff could simply walk from the school. In many cases, however, this is not possible, so school officials will also have to include plans for quickly mobilizing school district transportation in crisis situations to get students and staff to the alternative site if it is impractical or impossible to release kids directly from the school. (If students can logistically be released, accounting for all of these students, whose custody they are released to, and how this is verified and approved all remain as major planning issues.)

In some areas, it may be most practical for school transportation buses to be the initial holding site for students upon evacuation. This may especially be true in areas experiencing adverse weather conditions (e.g., freezing temperatures, snowstorms, or heavy rain) during the time of the crisis incident.

School officials may also wish to establish a secondary alternative site in the event that the first alternative site is unavailable or if the first alternative site is also the scene of a crisis situation. If at all possible, both primary and secondary alternative evacuation sites should *not* be other schools, because the evacuation of children and staff from one school to another could cause increased risks for disruptions, along with a possible transfer of psychological trauma, to the students and staff of the alternative site. Unfortunately, school officials may be unable to locate nonschool alternative sites; if required to use other schools, officials should have steps in their crisis guidelines for providing an adequate level of supervision and mental health support to everyone involved, including those students and staff at the receiving site.

Crisis planners should also prepare for the worst-case scenario of not being able to return immediately to their home school. This could occur as a result of damage to physical facilities, extended declaration of the school as a crime scene, or other unforeseen reasons. Plans for long-term continuity of educational services should therefore be included in school crisis guidelines.

Lockdown Procedures. The school shootings of the late 1990s brought new meaning to the word *lockdown* in schools. Lockdown drills were established in a number of schools in response to concerns about the need to clear students and staff quickly from the hallways and to move them to safer areas away from a potential security threat. Unfortunately, as a result of media attention and many misunderstandings, the term was perceived by many to be punitive, associated with the concept of prison lockdowns, or reminiscent of the nuclear and bomb drills practiced by many of the adults who now are working in schools or are parents of schoolchildren.

In reality, a lockdown is, in essence, a reverse fire drill. The purpose of a fire drill is to get students and staff safely out of harm's way by relocating them outside of the school. Students and staff become proficient and efficient in doing so through practice. The purpose of a lockdown is to get students and staff safely out of harm's way by relocating them out of the hallways and as far away from harm as possible within the school building. Typically, this means inside locked classrooms or other secure areas. Students and staff become proficient and efficient in doing so through practice. There is really nothing more—or less—to a lockdown.

Basic procedures for a typical lockdown generally include the following:

1. Use direct commands to indicate a lockdown, not codes. Code words or phrases are typically known to students anyway, especially if school officials communicate effectively the importance of lockdown procedures, so there really is no need to be secretive. (Even if you did want to be secretive, chances are good that the students would find out the meaning of the code in no time at all anyway!) Substitutes, parents, and other legitimate visitors, however, may very well be the only ones who would not know the meaning of the code word or phrase, yet school officials would want them to be safe and secure from harm's way in a legitimate crisis. By using a directive, such as, "We are in a lockdown situation. Everyone clear the halls and follow lockdown procedures immediately," even someone unfamiliar with the lockdown procedure would have a greater chance of getting to safety (or at least asking someone who knows how to do so) than they would if the code phrase for a lockdown was, "All staff members please help locate the custodian's flashlight," as it was in one elementary school. In that case, even the majority of the regular teachers forgot the code, and came out in the hallway to see who had the custodian's flashlight!

2. Students should go to the first available room, preferably with an adult present.

3. Staff should be assigned to clear students and staff from areas such as cafeterias and gymnasiums, and move them to the nearest secure location (e.g., a classroom or locker room), if possible. If such areas cannot be safely cleared, students and staff should be told to minimize their physical exposure, such as by dropping down to the ground, and to find available cover, such as behind a wall or table.

4. Secure windows, doors, and other entrances into the room.

5. Do not cover windows and doors. Note, however, that this is still an area of debate, even among some law enforcement officials. Arguments for covering doors and windows tend to support the idea that the potential offender will not be able to see inside. Arguments for keeping windows and doors clear include that this allows public safety officials to see what is occurring inside, and that requiring someone to pull shades could put them in greater jeopardy by having them stand in front of the doors and windows as they do so. Although I concur with those who support leaving shades up and keeping doors and windows clear, it is recommended that school officials confer with their local law enforcement representatives to ensure that they all agree on this issue.

6. Turn off all lights.

7. Move as far away from the doors and windows as soon as possible.

8. Minimize physical exposure and, if appropriate, seek protective cover.

9. Remain calm and absolutely quiet.

10. Wait for an "all clear" from an established or credible source.

One of the most important steps is to remain calm and absolutely quiet. In one lockdown drill that I observed, the majority of classrooms followed the established procedures perfectly. In one classroom, however, the students were not taking the process seriously, and that noise—and, in turn, their physical presence—was quickly and easily detected by those of us who could have been the "bad guys" out in the hall. Unfortunately, the students did not take the process seriously because their teacher did not treat the drill seriously, allowing the students to carry on conversations during the drill.

Educators have a number of questions about lockdowns that are difficult, if not impossible, for another person to answer. Some questions that school officials must ask of themselves, and that only they can answer, include the following:

- Can the doors to my classroom be locked? If yes, how? Do I leave them locked all of the time? If no, then what do I do?

- What other levels of protection are available if my doors will not lock?

- What other safe places are in my immediate area in the event that I cannot get to my room?

- If I need to communicate information, can I safely get to a phone? What other options exist if no phone is available?

- If kids or someone else I know knocks on my door demanding entry for their safety after I have shut it for the lockdown, do I open the door or do I let them stay outside? What if the person knocking is really the person who poses a danger?

These and other questions will ultimately have to be answered by the individuals asking them. No consultant or "expert," and especially no individual who is unfamiliar with the school, can answer these questions for someone else.

These lockdown suggestions are just that: suggestions. School officials and crisis team members should confer with their local public safety officials in developing specific lockdown guidelines, as well as evacuation and other guidelines, to ensure that the procedures they establish are consistent with local public safety expectations and recommendations, and with circumstances or conditions unique to their school and/or to their community.

Roles, Communications, and Counseling

As previously noted, crisis guideline components should include the roles and responsibilities of various individuals, a detailed communications plan, and a section devoted to counseling and mental health. Roles that should be included in the crisis guideline document are discussed in detail in Chapter 8. Communications and counseling issues are discussed in greater depth in Chapter 9. These areas, however, should be included in the crisis guidelines document, as referenced above.

Sharing Crisis Guideline Information

School and emergency service officials should certainly have copies of school crisis guidelines. But should they also be provided to students? To parents? To the media?

School and safety officials should communicate appropriate information on safety and crisis guidelines to students, parents, and the community. However, this does not automatically equate to disseminating printed copies of the full plan. Although students, parents, and the community should know that crisis guidelines exist and should know the reason why they exist, the specific portions and details of the crisis guidelines should be issued on a need-to-know basis as they relate to the roles and expectations of the particular individuals.

For example, students should know what is expected of them in a lockdown. Parents should know what is expected of them if a crisis takes place at their school. However, it would typically be inappropriate to provide the detailed logistics and implementation of the full set of overall crisis guidelines to everyone.

The Preparation

Getting the crisis teams together and developing crisis guideline documents are only part of the preparation to be done for crisis situations. Crisis preparedness planning is a process, and knowledgeable crisis planners realize that the only time that preparing for a crisis really ends is when they retire from their job! A number of preparatory tasks are listed below.

Establish Command Posts and Staging Areas

School officials, in cooperation with public safety agencies, should identify multiple sites that can serve as a command post from which crisis management could be coordinated in the event of an incident. The reason for having multiple designated sites is so that backup locations are identified in the event that the primary site is the actual scene of the crisis or otherwise inappropriate for use based on crisis circumstances. Potential sites may include the principal's conference room, a library, or, if the site needs to be outside, an athletic field office or other accessible, but safe, location.

Depending on the size and resources of the school district, it might very well be appropriate to have a mobile crisis command center. Perhaps an old school bus, mobile classroom, or delivery vehicle could be equipped with the necessary resources and equipment to serve as a mobile location site for managing a school crisis. Additionally, it might be wise, especially in larger school districts, to have a dedicated command center at the school district's headquarters, adequately equipped with such items as phones, two-way radios, and maps so that school leaders unable to respond on-site to the school crisis can be centrally located to coordinate communications and decisions in a timely and efficient manner.

Staging areas should also be identified in advance for use by SWAT teams and other emergency service providers (including for multijurisdiction coordination); for use in medical triage, media and press conferences, mental health and related psychological services, and other functions as needed; and for use, if necessary, as command posts.

Create Family Reunification Sites and Procedures

Parents are one of the few groups of people who are likely to arrive on scene at a school crisis faster than, or at least as fast as, the media is. Parents will often understandably want to remove their child from the school as quickly as possible, at least until control has been regained. Although it is important for students and staff to return to normalcy as quickly as possible, school officials may find it necessary or prudent to reunite students and parents—and, for that matter, staff and their families—as the crisis unfolds.

School and safety officials will be poised most effectively to manage a school crisis if they have a designated location off-site and away from the crisis location itself. If a crisis is small-scale in nature, a designated location in another wing or adjacent building of the school may suffice. However, in the

event of a larger-scale incident or an ongoing active scenario, a location totally off-site may be much more appropriate and necessary, especially because traffic flow typically becomes overwhelmingly congested and phone
systems tend to overload and shut down in a major incident.

School officials should have identified methods in their crisis communications plans for directing parents to reunification sites immediately upon
the decision to relocate students to these sites. Crisis guidelines should include steps for sending crisis team members to the reunification sites, along
with student emergency information data, student release cards, communications equipment, and other necessary items described in the emergency
kits below. Parents should be encouraged during the crisis to avoid visiting
the regular school site and to avoid calling the regular school or using cell
phones so that they do not tie up lines or overload communications systems.

Crisis guidelines for the parent center should involve adequate staffing,
including counselors and mental health personnel, at least one school official from the crisis team with decision-making authority, and adequate staff
to handle student and parent intake, phone calls, media liaison, and related
functions. Because a presumably large number of individuals will be relocating from the crisis scene to this center, it will, in essence, operate much like
the command site where the actual crisis is taking place. It is therefore important to have advance arrangements for use of this site and a thorough
knowledge of communications capabilities (e.g., phone, fax, and e-mail) and
other logistical needs.

Prepare for Medical Emergencies

Most schools are fortunate if they have one school nurse. They are especially lucky if that nurse is on-site at the same school each day of the week on
a full-time basis. Relying on the school nurse to handle all medical emergencies in a crisis, particularly if there are mass injuries, is totally unrealistic.

Some steps that can be taken to prepare better for medical needs in an
emergency include

- Identifying school staff members interested in being trained as first
  responders in a crisis situation, and providing them with at least a basic training session and necessary updates on first aid, CPR, and related medical safety techniques
- Maintaining a list of individuals who have received first responder
  training, and including a copy in the crisis guidelines
- Ensuring that school nurses (if the school is fortunate enough to have
  such persons) have had training comparable to emergency-room
  level trauma preparation so that they are best prepared for managing
  a school crisis
- Designating a location or locations on the school grounds where a
  medical helicopter could land in the event that one is needed to
  life-flight injured individuals to hospitals (although this need may exist anywhere, school officials in rural or remote areas in particular

should prepare for such support because they are often far from a hospital)

- Placing first aid kits in various locations inside and outside of the school building, as well as on each school bus, so that they are easily accessible in a crisis; ensuring that crisis team members and others on staff know where these kits are located; and perhaps including a list of these locations in the crisis guideline document

- Creating a method for identifying individuals sent to the hospital when there are mass injuries: for example, using wristbands on which individual names can be written in indelible ink

- Determining which hospital or hospitals would be used in the event of mass injuries, and which school representatives will go to these hospitals to identify injured students and/or staff in a crisis situation

- Identifying a way for student emergency records to be accessed by authorized school officials during a crisis, and determining how these will be made available if they are needed to authorize medical treatment for a student whose parent cannot be contacted

Assemble Critical Facility and Tactical Information

The more information that police and public safety agencies have available on the school physical plant and its operations, the better tactical advantage they will have in carrying out search, rescue, and related crisis functions. School officials and their fellow crisis team members, including public safety representatives, should consider the following suggestions:

1. Provide police, fire, and other appropriate emergency service agencies with a copy of the blueprints for all schools. An important reminder: before turning over blueprints, school officials should ensure that they are up-to-date and accurate. A number of school officials have been rushing to turn over building blueprints, but have forgotten to check that the blueprints being given to public safety officials accurately reflect building layouts after years of new construction, remodeling, and other changes.

2. Invite police, fire, and other public safety agencies to the school to discuss safety concerns and to allow them to take a walk-through of the facility so that they may become familiar with it.

3. Make the school building and grounds accessible at night and on weekends for police SWAT teams (and other public safety agencies) to train there and even on a school bus so that they become familiar with these environments.

4. Consider requiring contractors, especially those hired for new construction where you can build this into their contracts, to produce school blueprints and other facility schematic plans on CD-ROM so that they can easily be accessed on a laptop computer.

5. Number, letter, and/or color code both the inside and outside of doors to help public service agencies easily identify and reference entry and exit points in a crisis.

6. Create a tactical resource listing of the following locations and information, and provide this information (updated yearly) to public safety agencies serving the school:

- Power main panels and electrical closets, controls, and the like
- Water, gas, electric, and related utility controls and main leads, along with the names and phone numbers for the companies supplying such services
- Telephone control boxes
- Information on alarms, bells, sprinklers, and related systems
- Location of high-risk or critical areas within the school, such as day care centers and areas dedicated to special needs children (i.e., physically disabled, special education, and other students with special needs)
- Information on HVAC (Heating, Ventilation, and Air Conditioning) system and controls
- Location of security cameras and other devices
- Main computer circuits and operational controls
- Remote shut-off locations for utilities and alarms
- Locations of hazardous materials, flammable materials, chemistry labs and supply rooms, or similar sites
- Locations of elevators, false ceilings, electrical and other ducts, crawl spaces, and utility access points
- Location of all fire extinguishers, first aid equipment, and other necessary supplies
- Emergency telephone, pager, cell phone, or other numbers for crisis team members, maintenance and other facility plant supervisors, and outside utility companies, security or other systems officials, and related contractors

7. Take still photographs of key areas within the school, such as the office area, common areas, and chemistry labs, and, if possible, do a videotaped tour of the school, including office areas, common areas, hallways and stairwells, labs, boiler rooms and custodial areas, and other critical areas.

8. Take aerial photographs of the school, its campus, and surrounding neighborhoods, and have these blown up in size and made available for use in identifying access and evacuation routes.

9. Consider establishing secured boxes immediately outside of school buildings containing access keys to the building for emergency service personnel. Also consider providing a set of school master keys (to buildings, classrooms, and lockers) to the local police department to be kept in the car

of each shift's patrol commander, along with other tactical information listed in this section. A similar set of keys should be made available to the school crisis incident manager.

Identify the Location and Needs of Special Student Populations

Crisis guidelines should include steps for making sure that the needs of special student populations are met during a crisis. These populations may include physically disabled students, special education students, or other unique groups, such as children in a high school day care center or preschool children at an elementary school. These students are likely to require additional support, especially during evacuations and other drills.

Develop Systems for Accounting for Students, Staff, and Others

School officials need to develop plans for checking attendance and accounting for students, staff, substitutes, and volunteers, during a time of crisis, evacuation, or lockdown. Schools should also have the ability to generate absentee lists for the day quickly. The last thing needed during a crisis is to have people attempting to track down a "missing" student who had never showed up at the school in the first place.

Prepare and Maintain Emergency Kits

School officials should assemble emergency kits for use in crisis situations, especially when an evacuation is required. Each crisis team member should have a kit, and additional kits could be placed in multiple strategic locations within the school and in designated areas outside of the school, such as in the trunk of the police shift commander's patrol car, at the school district's central office, and at local police and fire departments.

School leaders for the St. Vrain Valley School District in Colorado created a unique name for their crisis response team and their emergency kits. The district's crisis team is referred to as the DIRT (District Incident Response Team) team, and the bags containing their crisis kits are called—of course—DIRT bags. These names have stuck in the minds of adults and kids alike, and the district, lead by its public information coordinator, Nancy Herbert, and with the strong support of its superintendent and board, has made safety an ongoing priority through various strategies—the DIRT team and DIRT bags being only two of their many crisis preparedness initiatives.

According to Nancy Herbert (personal communication, November 13, 1999), their DIRT bags contain, in part, the following items: a first aid kit, including latex gloves; a small tool kit; a box of index cards for student release; a book of floor plans to give to the incident commander; a list of staff members, including substitutes, and their emergency contacts; a large water bottle; a space blanket; crackers and juice (in case of sugar imbalance); the crisis plan; a cell phone/two-way radio, backup batteries, and a list of cell phone numbers for crisis team members; a photo ID; a vest and cap with the DIRT logo to identity them as crisis team members; and other necessary materials.

Building administrators and district DIRT team members are to have DIRT bags available at all times.

All school officials should create emergency crisis kits. These kits should be located at strategic sites, such as in administrative offices, in the departments or vehicle trunks of emergency service responders, at reunification sites, and other key locations. Items to consider including are

- A list of the trained medical first responders on staff
- Communications equipment, including extra cell phones and backup batteries
- A bullhorn
- School district and emergency response telephone directories for the school and community
- A student directory with address, telephone, and parent contract information
- A staff directory with home and emergency contacts
- Student health and emergency records
- Telephone numbers, including cell phone numbers, fax numbers, and e-mail information, for crisis team members, staff, and other support services
- A list of phone trees
- Floor plans and tactical information
- Bus routes, numbers, and contact information
- Yearbooks, student IDs, or other photos
- Attendance rosters
- Pens, markers, paper, name tags, and related materials
- Prefabricated signs, with such messages as *PARENTS, COUNSELORS, VOLUNTEERS, POLICE, MEDICAL, MEDIA, KEEP OUT, NEED HELP,* and other appropriate messages
- Flashlights, tape, tools, and related equipment
- A laptop computer and printer, if possible (a small copy machine might also be located at reunification sites, alternate sites, and other locations outside of the crisis scene)

School officials can certainly add items within reason as they deem appropriate, and it is understandable that not everyone will be able to have or to carry all of these items. Technology should be utilized, if at all possible, so that the records, photos, and other items are available on CD-ROM and can be accessed via laptop computers. (Of course, this means that backup batteries and computer supplies would be needed!)

Assess and Enhance Communications Capabilities

School officials should thoroughly evaluate their communications capability and, if necessary, invest in timely improvements. Questions for evaluation should include the following:

- Are there phones in classrooms or, if not, at least in each wing of the building so that teachers and staff can easily call the office or 911?

- Can school officials communicate to and from portable classroom trailers?

- Are there an adequate number of functional two-way radio units to allow communication among the school administrators, school security or school resource officer, secretary, custodian, and staff who take students outside for physical education class or elementary recess? Are those units and their backup batteries kept charged and accessible?

- Can a mechanism be created to allow faster and more direct communications between school and law enforcement personnel, such as through a shared two-way radio frequency?

- Are there charged bullhorns available in the event that a crisis requires crisis team members to communicate clearly and effectively with large groups of students in hallways or outside of the school?

- Are there dedicated, private phone lines available at the school that are separate from the main phone system?

- Does the phone system have caller ID or automatic return calling services to help identify incoming calls? Is there a mechanism for tracking internal calls within the district?

- What support can the telephone service provider offer in tracing bomb threats and other threatening calls?

- Are there cellular phones available at each school for use in a crisis? Are backup batteries kept charged and accessible?

- If school officials have access to computers and e-mail from school offices and classrooms, does the 911 dispatch center (or local police department) have e-mail also so that e-mail messages can be sent from individual classrooms or offices where phone communications may not be possible?

- Do crisis team members have timely and adequate access to bilingual communicators remotely and on-site?

- Does the school have cable TV and internal TV broadcast abilities? Can these be remotely controlled?

- Are computer hubs within the school and/or district accessible? Are they adequately secured?

- Can the school's website be used to disseminate information to parents, community members, the media, and other interested parties?

- Do schools have broadcast fax, voice mail, and e-mail capabilities for sending mass communications in a crisis?

- Is there a voice mail line that can be used to call in for updated information?

- Does the school system have a master record of telephone companies and account representatives for local, long distance, cellular, Internet, and other communications? If these services are not all provided by the same company, then are school officials aware of the difference in vendors?
- Is there a specific individual within the school district responsible for coordinating communications systems? Does this individual coordinate information with school safety and technology officials?
- Have school safety and public safety officials shared information on these and other communications capabilities?

School officials should also have staff and parent phone trees available for use during a crisis. Notifying all school staff and parents in a timely manner at a time of crisis is critical to crisis management.

A mechanism should also be established to create and maintain open phone lines from school district headquarters to school crisis sites and command posts. In other words, once a connection is made between two points, these lines should be left open, even when they are not being actively used, so that callers do not have to redial and risk encountering busy or overloaded communications lines. Charged backup batteries that provide for the extended use of cell phones, vehicle adapters, and such other items can help extend the life of cell phone batteries.

Fortunately, new technology presents us with hope for continuing improvements in preparing for crisis situations. Digital imagining, for example, could be used to store student photos on CD-ROMs, which could then, if necessary, be used in a laptop computer to identify students at hospitals or elsewhere outside of the school environment in a crisis.

Evaluate Public Safety Capabilities in Advance

Police, fire, and emergency medical personnel have historically had little training related to school safety and little exposure to school settings. Trends in school violence in the late 1990s also shifted the way tactical teams approach their need to secure areas, moving away from only setting up and securing a perimeter to actually conducting a search and rescue because of the presence of active shooters. The ability to control alarms so that emergency service personnel can hear voices and noises, the familiarity tactical officers have with school stairs and hallways, knowledge of how entrances and locks work, and similar information can all aid in an effective tactical response to a school crisis.

Law enforcement officials face some particular challenges, including the fact that

- Difficulties in processing large crime scenes can easily occur when there is a serious incident at a school, especially if a significant portion of the school is designated as a crime scene

- Hundreds of victim, witness, and suspect interviews may have to be conducted

- Coordinating the transfer of command and/or the smooth interaction between incident commanders from different agencies involved in a school crisis can, at times, be difficult

- They need to deal with media information, rumor control, and related issues

- They need to reduce dangers created by media helicopters broadcasting live from around the crisis area; in fact, law enforcement officials may want to investigate the feasibility of contacting the Federal Aviation Administration to request clearance of air space around the crisis site, especially if it is a prolonged situation

- Greater confusion can occur if the lead agency is a small department with few officers; mutual aid pacts and logistical agreements can help reduce some of the confusion

Another difficulty centers on the common inability of police, fire, and emergency medical personnel to communicate on the same two-way radio frequency in a crisis. Although a number of agencies have been working to improve these communications issues, it would appear that the problem still exists in many communities. Public safety officials, along with school personnel, need to assess their communications capabilities during a crisis and to move toward closing gaps in communications. Nobody can afford to have public safety and school professionals running messages back and forth while chaos is growing all around them.

Assess Traffic Flow and Evacuation Routes

School and public safety officials should examine traffic routes in and out of schools to determine how they can contain overflow in a crisis, maintain clear access for emergency service vehicles, and still facilitate an anticipated rush from parents, media, and others to the scene. Unfortunately, if they are not careful, emergency service vehicles themselves can contribute greatly to the problem. Use of aerial photographs and maps can help in the assessment, as well as in an actual incident response.

Officials may wish to install gates at the driveway entrances to schools so that that they can at least attempt to block off an onslaught of vehicles in an emergency situation. Parking lot design, routine traffic routes that split parent drivers from school buses, and other traffic flow considerations should also be taken into consideration.

Develop Strategies to Address Transportation Needs

School transportation services can play a major role in school crisis situations. A number of steps can be taken to better prepare for transportation-related crisis services and needs:

- Develop an action plan for quickly mobilizing school bus drivers during off-peak driving times, such as during the middle of the school day, so that a mechanism is in place for obtaining an adequate fleet response to such crisis situations as evacuations or transports to alternative sites.

- Equip all buses with two-way communications systems that adequately cover districtwide use. Consider multiple channels, one of which can be designated an emergency-only channel, and discuss communications procedures in a crisis situation.

- Equip drivers who go on field trips or special events with cell phones.

- Ensure that drivers have student rosters, student emergency data, and first aid kits.

- Train drivers to increase awareness of student behavior management strategies, security threat trends and procedures, and crisis preparedness guidelines, including procedures for school evacuations, relocation to alternative sites, and so forth.

- Provide law enforcement agencies an opportunity to use school buses for tactical training exercises.

- Consider putting the bus number in large numbers on the top of the bus unit so that it could be identified from a police helicopter.

- Make sure that all bus units have the name of the school district clearly displayed.

- Place signs on all sides of the bus unit requesting that, in an emergency, passersby first notify 911, and then a designated number at the school district.

- Have drivers conduct periodic bus evacuations.

- Consider having backup drivers for emergencies, and create a list of school employees who do not normally drive, but who have a license to drive, a school bus. (School officials may consider having some additional individuals, such as crisis team members, trained as bus drivers for emergency situations.)

Remember that school bus drivers are typically the first and last school employee to see children each day. Their training and involvement in school security and crisis preparedness planning is critical to having a successful safe schools strategy.

Portable Classrooms, Open Classrooms, and Other Sites

Growing school populations and limited space are plaguing a number of schools across the country in terms of safety issues. Portable classrooms (i.e., trailers) typically have no public address systems, no phones, no fire or other alarms, and other communications gaps. Evacuation procedures, lockdowns, and other crisis guideline implementation could easily be hampered in these areas, and special consideration should be given to portable classrooms when enhancing physical security measures and developing crisis guidelines.

Open classroom areas, shared space rooms, and similar arrangements also present unique conditions for safety planning. Oftentimes, there are few places to seek shelter in these areas, and securing a room or rooms is frequently almost impossible. When these types of design exist in schools, options for relocation in the general area of such rooms, methods for obtaining protective cover and minimizing physical exposure, and other risk reduction measures should be examined closely as you develop crisis guidelines.

Risk reduction options should be closely examined when these designs exist.

After-School Programs, Special Events, and More

Crisis team members must also recognize that crises are not confined to certain times or places. After-school programs, special events such as athletic events and dances, adult education sites, and field trips are all subject to experiencing a crisis situation. Security staffing and other adult supervision, access control, communications capabilities and procedures, coordination with public safety agencies, and a number of other logistical considerations for handling crises at these locations and in such nontraditional school settings as alternative schools should also be included in the crisis preparedness planning process.

Training and Exercising the Guidelines

Crisis preparedness guidelines should be tested and revised as appropriate. In addition, all staff should be trained on the guidelines. Furthermore, the importance of following adult directions and the overall importance of safety-related drills should be communicated to students.

Testing crisis guidelines does not automatically equate to a full-dress simulation. Tabletop scenarios alone can help school and other safety officials identify a number of gaps in their guidelines. Furthermore, full simulations, as long as they are conducted with volunteers and the fact that it is a simulation has been made clearly known to all in advance, should also not be objectionable, because both school and law enforcement officials typically learn a great deal as a result of these exercises.

Pulling It All Together

It should be clear that preparing for crisis situations is an ongoing process, not a one-time event. Effective planning takes time and is extremely detail oriented. The degree of success school and public safety officials can have in managing a crisis, however, is directly related to their degree of preparation.

8

Managing Crisis Incidents

No matter how much you do to prevent a crisis incident, one can still occur. When the chaos is over and the dust has settled, the first question asked is going to be whether the situation could have been prevented. The majority of the questions thereafter are going to focus on how well prepared you were to manage those situations you could not prevent.

Chapter 7 highlighted the crisis preparedness process, the development of written guideline documents, and a number of things that can be done to prepare for managing a crisis. If the majority of preparedness steps listed in Chapter 7 have been taken before an actual incident occurs, school crisis team members are likely to find that the management of the incident will flow much more smoothly than the traditional approach of "flying by the seat of your pants." To avoid repetition, this chapter will cover additional thoughts on managing crisis incidents with the assumption that crisis team members will already have put in place those items discussed in Chapter 7.

Crisis Response: The First Half Hour

You hear the shots. You answer the call for help. You have heard the most dreaded message a school official will ever hear: *"Shots have been fired in the cafeteria."*

Now what? Where do you go, and what do you do first?

There are four priorities in the initial response to a school crisis. A half hour is used here as a reference to help people put tasks in a time frame and to grasp what should be done and when it should be done. The reality, however, is that a response to these four priority areas may run from the first minutes up to hours into the crisis, depending on the nature of the situation.

These four areas are not ranked, nor are they necessarily chronological in order of occurrence. In fact, under ideal circumstances, they would all be occurring simultaneously. Top priorities should include

1. *Securing all students, staff, and legitimate visitors.* Depending on the crisis, this may involve an evacuation, a lockdown, or both simultaneously. The focus should be on making sure that all students, staff, and others are legitimately out of harm's way.

2. *Assisting the injured.* Time is of the essence in a medical emergency. In some cases, minutes or even seconds can make a difference between life and death. The steps recommended in Chapter 7 for preparing for medical emergencies should help school officials reduce potential losses by strengthening their capacity to provide a timely and effective response to medical emergencies.

3. *Requesting assistance.* The first call for assistance should be to police, fire, and/or emergency medical services, all typically done by calling 911 in many areas. Amazingly, we have seen delays by school officials in obtaining assistance because they chose to call the superintendent or other central office officials before requesting outside emergency assistance. Although the importance of having top school leaders informed of what is going on cannot be overlooked, it is unlikely that the superintendent is also a police officer, firefighter, or medical technician able to provide direct services to students and staff. Get the call out for outside emergency assistance first, then notify designated central office officials who can help mobilize resources within the district and other outside support in addition to the emergency service providers already contacted.

4. *Engaging crisis team members and crisis guidelines.* This is where the crisis guideline development, training, and related preparation will be put to the real test. Although you will want to make sure that all of the elements of the crisis guidelines are being followed, some of the most important subcategories in this area should include the following actions:

- Secure the crime scene. This is a phrase well understood by law enforcement, but commonly unknown to or misunderstood by most educators. It is a very important step in the criminal investigation process, however. It short, it means protecting the area where the crisis occurred from tampering, movement, or other disruption until the police arrive. It is so important that it is discussed in more detail below.

- Verify facts and begin documentation. Once control is regained, crisis team members should focus on verifying facts as quickly as possible and documenting these facts as they are obtained. It is suggested that each crisis team have at least one individual who serves as the recorder and focuses exclusively on documenting the crisis and the responses to it.

- Determine the status of the remaining school day. If the crisis occurs before school dismissals, educators will quickly have to determine whether or not school will remain open for the remainder of the school day. Factors to consider in this decision are discussed in more detail below.

- Activate the communications plan. School officials typically equate a communications plan with dealing with the media. Although the media is one area that should be addressed by a crisis communications plan, it is certainly not the only one. Components of a crisis communications plan are discussed in more detail in Chapter 9.

Although there are only four categories suggested for the first response phase, there are many subcategories and considerations under each of these areas. In fact, to be able to complete everything that needs to be done under each of these in one half hour is highly unlikely, especially in a major crisis. By focusing on these areas first, however, crisis responders will be better able to prioritize the many things that they will need to do over the length of the crisis.

Securing Crime Scenes and Preserving Evidence

In lay terms, securing the crime scene basically means protecting the area where the crisis took place and preventing the movement, contamination, destruction, or alteration of evidence. This typically means restricting access to the area and prohibiting items from being moved, removed, or touched. Such items might include, for example, shell casings from discharged weapons, firearms, knives, or the personal property of a shooter or victim.

Securing the area also means *not* cleaning up crisis outcomes, such as blood on the floor (something that educators by nature rush to do, typically to prevent someone from stepping in it, slipping, or simply having to see it) or bullet holes in the wall. Again, this is done by setting up some type of perimeter around the scene of the incident until police arrive; for example, you might block off access all the way around the crime scene with tape or rope (make sure, however, that the person securing the crime scene is also not contaminating it by doing so). Assigning an individual or several individuals on the crisis team responsibility for securing the crime scene would be a wise thing to do.

Only police officials should be allowed access, and once they take over the crime scene, they will typically assume responsibility for it unless they indicate otherwise. Until that time—and, for that matter, usually after that time as well—school officials, parents, media, and all others, including superintendents, board members, crisis team members, and other ranking officials, must be required to remain outside the crime scene perimeter regardless of their title or authority. The only exception, however, would likely be those rendering medical assistance to victims who cannot be removed from the crime scene area.

Although a school cafeteria or classroom may be the crime scene in smaller crisis situations, the entire school could very well be designated a crime scene in others depending on the circumstances. Designating the entire school a crime scene has not only been an effective way to preserve evidence and avoid crime scene contamination, but has also served as a way to help keep media, parents, and others away from the area until the situation is brought under control and the investigators have had an opportunity to make an initial assessment of the scene. It is also easier to designate a larger area than necessary as the crime scene and eventually scale it down than it is to start small and try to expand it at a later time.

It would be prudent for crisis team members, if not the entire school staff, to receive an in-service presentation by their local law enforcement agency on how to secure a crime scene and how to preserve evidence.

Deciding Whether to Close School

School leaders will need to decide on whether or not school will remain open shortly after the incident has unfolded. Poland and McCormick (1999) identify several factors to consider when deciding this issue:

- Emotional support will be needed for the individuals involved in the crisis, and, in general, staff and students who experienced the crisis should be kept together. Exceptions include very young students, such as kindergartners, who should be reunited with the parents or guardians.
- Sending students home would allow staff to dedicate their full attention to managing the crisis and its aftermath.
- The police investigation time, damage to the school, complications with transportation issues, and unsupervised children may require an early closure.
- Parents may wish for their children to go home with them, and this could affect attendance and the processing of the crisis incident.
- The majority of staff members will need to have control of their own emotions in order to assist the students, and if the majority of them are unable to do so, closing school may be a necessity.
- If school remains open, staff will need to know what type of bell schedule to follow. It would typically be appropriate under these circumstances to allow students to stay in one class, such as the one they were in at the time of the incident or their homeroom, until they have had adequate time to deal with the crisis.

Poland and McCormick note that the general recommendation, providing that circumstances allow it, is to keep children in school so that they can receive care and support in coping with the crisis. Even in situations where school is closed the day of the incident, they stress that "your goal should be to return your students to school at some location as quickly as possible—preferably the next day—so that they can receive the assistance of trained school personnel and to decrease the occurrence of 'school phobia' among students" (p. 72).

Roles and Responsibilities

Responding to serious incidents on a regular basis is the job of police, fire, medical, and other emergency service personnel—not school officials. School personnel must, however, know what their roles and responsibilities will be during a crisis even though it is not a part of their daily job routine. Knowing and understanding their roles in a crisis situation, as well as knowing the systems used by many emergency service providers in responding to serious incidents, will help school crisis team members and their fellow staff members better respond in an actual incident.

Incident Command System (ICS)

The Incident Command System (ICS) originated as the result of organizational problems, including ineffective communications, lack of accountability, and undefined command structure, identified from multi-agency responses to major wildland fires in Southern California in the 1970s. ICS was adopted by the National Fire Academy (NFA) to standardize the responses of individual agencies working on the common goal of protecting life, property, and the environment through command, control, and coordination. ICS eventually evolved into an all-risk incident management system for all types of fire and nonfire emergencies (Federal Emergency Management Agency [FEMA], 1995).

ICS is based on the business management practices of planning, directing, organizing, coordinating, communicating, delegating, and evaluating, and relies on having functional areas for managing serious incidents. Command is responsible for the overall incident management, and may be a single command, where one commander is responsible for incident management, or a unified command, where several individuals appointed by their respective departments jointly determine the incident management strategy. According to FEMA (1995), an effective ICS will include an all-risk system and suitability for use with any type of jurisdiction or agency, and will be adaptable to all incidents regardless of size, all users, and new technology.

FEMA (1995) identifies the eight components of an ICS as the following:

1. *Common terminology* to prevent confusion through the use of an incident name and common terms for personnel, equipment, facilities, and procedures

2. *Modular organization* through the use of an expandable top-down structure, with size depending on the incident's management needs

3. *Integrated communications* using a communications system with common terminology, standard operating procedures, common frequencies, and so forth

4. *Unified command structure,* whether single or unified, as described above

5. *Consolidated action plans,* including verbal or written (especially if multiple agencies are involved) plans of strategic goals, objectives, and activities

6. *A manageable span of control* of subordinates being supervised, generally from three to seven

7. *Designated incident facilities,* such as command posts and staging areas

8. *Comprehensive resource management,* including use of staging areas, consolidation resources, reduction of communication loads, and ongoing monitoring of resource status

The ICS functional areas include

1. *Command* function, responsible for overall on-scene management, includes an incident commander (IC) and, depending on the size or complexity of the incident, may include a safety officer to address hazardous or unsafe conditions, a liaison officer to coordinate with other agencies, and an information officer to deal with media and pubic information

2. *Operations* function, which is responsible for the actual tactical operations at the incident

3. *Planning* function in larger incidents, which includes the collection, evaluation, dissemination, and use of information on the incident development and status of resources

4. *Logistics* function, which is responsible for locating and organizing facilities, services, and materials needed to manage the incident, such as communications, medical support, and food

5. *Finance* function, which tracks costs and financial considerations associated with the incident management

It is important that school officials, especially crisis team members, understand that this structure may be in place and that the response of emergency service personnel from public safety agencies may operate following an ICS model. On the other hand, local emergency service officials may very well not be familiar with ICS. It would behoove school officials to confer with police, fire, and other emergency service providers during their crisis preparation stages to ascertain whether or not such a response model is used by the agencies and, if so, how the school system will respond in conjunction with such a protocol.

School System Interface With ICS

School officials may very likely find out that the roles and responsibilities of their crisis team members fall along the lines of ICS functional areas. It is unlikely, however, that school officials have conceptualized and formally structured their crisis guidelines to include roles and responsibilities in as detailed a structure as the ICS. Nevertheless, because school officials are the lead responders until public safety agencies arrive and because they will have to transfer information on their initial response to the responding personnel, they will need to know the form in which these agencies may be setting up and with whom school crisis team members might need to confer.

For example, ICS-like functions performed by school officials might include the following:

Command: The incident commander (IC) for the school district would likely be the superintendent, and his or her assistant commander would likely be a deputy or assistant superintendent. The school IC would likely have a risk management official fulfilling the safety officer functions and a public/community relations official performing the information officer function with media and other audiences. Depending on the size of the school district, the district's security director, school resource officer, or similar representative responsible for school safety might serve as liaison officer, coordinating with other public safety agencies.

Operations: The school district's representative leading the actual response to the crisis typically would be the building principal, possibly in conjunction with the school security coordinator or school resource officer, and/or members of the school crisis teams.

Planning: The school administrator in charge of student services (including such personnel as social workers, counselors, psychologists, nurses, and support programs staff) would be the most likely school official to fulfill the ICS planning role. This function might also be split among the superintendent, building principal, security official, and business manager, depending on the size of the district or nature of the crisis incident.

Logistics: Facilities, services, grounds, materials, food services, transportation, and perhaps even personnel would typically fall under the direction of the school business manager. Titles for this position may run from *assistant superintendent* to *coordinator*, depending on size of the district, but the functions are typically the same.

Finance: Financial issues are generally under the direction of a school treasurer and/or a financial director. These functions or positions sometimes fall under the control of the business manager, so it would not be unreasonable to see both finance and logistics fall under the supervision of one leader.

Based on this type of comparison, it would appear as though the superintendent, the principal of the school in crisis, the safety/security director, the student services director, the business manager, and the treasurer or financial director should play key roles in the overall incident command structure for the school district. These people, in turn, would also be central to the liaison with public safety incident commanders upon their arrival on the scene of the incident.

Specific Roles to Consider

School officials will have to evaluate their own organizational structure, their district and building positions and specialty areas, and related factors to determine which specific person or persons will perform which specific tasks (including those listed above and below, as well as the many others referenced in Chapters 7 and 9). It would be prudent for school officials to assign alternate or backup persons (perhaps at least two or three individuals deep for those mission-critical areas) to complete the emergency functions, as Murphy's Law tends to strike along with an actual crisis (e.g., the primary individual responsible for fulfilling a particular role could be off ill, out of town, at a conference, or elsewhere at the time of the incident). The following list highlights specific tasks undertaken by various personnel typically involved in school district crisis responses:

1. *Administrator-in-Charge:* The school superintendent, principal, or other administrator-in-charge should be responsible for

   - Assessing the situation, engaging appropriate crisis guidelines, and monitoring their implementation

   - Serving as the liaison with public safety agency ICs once they arrive, and coordinating with key individuals and organizations in the broader school community

   - Assigning duties as needed

   - Reviewing and approving public information releases, if possible

   - Approving appropriate requests for additional resources

2. *School Safety/Security Official:* School security or school police officials' roles may include

   - Assigning, supervising, and coordinating school security and/or police staff to supervise and control the incident site, perimeter, crowds, and access, and to direct traffic and escort visitors

   - Maintaining liaison with public safety agencies on operational issues

- Collecting, organizing, and documenting facts, statements, and information

- Briefing incident commanders and other key officials on investigations and security issues

- Other duties associated with the protection of life, property, and information

3. *Public Information Official:* Community and/or media relations personnel should

   - Engage and monitor implementation of the crisis communications plan

   - Coordinate appropriate media briefings and other incident-related communications briefings and information dissemination

   - Provide updated fact sheets for secretaries and other persons communicating with parents and the public

   - Ensure effective and consistent communications, in cooperation with school administrators, with the victims and their families

   - Maintain as detailed records as possible of the information requested and released

4. *Secretaries and Clerical Staff:* These individuals play a key role in the day-to-day operations of schools and will also play a key role in managing a crisis incident. Their roles should include

   - Having one designated secretary, if possible, on the crisis team to document the actions taken by school officials in managing the crisis

   - Coordinating requests for additional copying, supplies, and other such items needed to manage the incident

   - Maintaining a log of phone calls whenever possible

   - Utilizing fact sheets prepared for communications with parents, community members, and other callers

   - Referring media inquiries to the designated staff

   - *Not* speculating or giving opinions

   - *Not* releasing confidential student, staff, or other information

   - Limiting the use of office phones during an emergency, especially by students, strangers, and visitors

   - Knowing how to report emergencies (e.g., knowing what information 911 dispatchers will need to know and how it should be provided)

   - Having and making available updated quick resource reference lists, contact information, and so forth

- Knowing how to use, and coordinate the use of, broadcast fax, e-mail, voice mail, and other message systems, including pubic address systems and bell systems

5. *Teachers and Staff*: Their roles will include

   - Implementing evacuations, lockdowns, or other directives as issued by crisis management leaders
   - *Not* assuming that everything is secure and back to normal until given an "all clear" indication of such
   - Staying with and supervising students, with an emphasis on ensuring that they remain as calm and quiet as possible, and that they follow adult directions
   - Being prepared to take student roll and to report missing students
   - Knowing how to report concerns and needs related to the crisis, and knowing to whom to report them
   - Being familiar with, and prepared to deal with, student emotions and psychological reactions to the crisis
   - Being flexible and prepared to adapt curriculum and classroom activities in response to the crisis and, in particular, to help students process and manage their reactions to the crisis
   - Communicating clearly, concisely, and honestly to students before, during, and after the crisis

6. *Counselors, Psychologists, Social Workers, and Other Mental Health Professionals*: These personnel should

   - Mobilize all available mental health resource personnel and materials from within, and if necessary from outside of, the school district
   - Establish and coordinate group and individual counseling opportunities for students, teachers, staff, and others, including self-referral systems
   - Identify resources for teachers, parents, and others to help identify the natural progression and management of the grief and healing process
   - Coordinate debriefings and make services available to those providing care and management of the crisis
   - Identify resources for parents and the broader community to deal with grief and healing
   - Prepare for memorial services, and for the long-term support needed for anniversary dates of the crisis incidents
   - Implement a comprehensive communication plan for making available services known

- Maintain adequate records of services provided

7. *Custodians and Maintenance Personnel:* Their role will include
   - Assisting in physically securing buildings and grounds, or, when appropriate, providing access to normally secured areas for crisis management officials
   - Being available to brief public safety responders on building design and operations
   - Having information available on emergency shut-off controls for utilities, alarms, bells, and so forth
   - Being prepared for requests to assist in providing additional special needs, such as additional electrical, mechanical, and other resources
   - Preparing for quick mobilization of staff for major clean-up, repair, and other activities at the appropriate time as directed by incident commanders

8. *Transportation Staff:* Such staff, including bus drivers, can play critical roles, including
   - Being available and flexible for short-notice emergency transportation needs
   - Becoming familiar with alternate site plans, evacuation routes and procedures, and so forth
   - Knowing how properly to use and maintain two-way radio communications equipment
   - Having first aid kits and related supplies on buses at all times
   - Maintaining rosters and emergency contact information for regular riders
   - Reporting weather or other emergency conditions, obstacles, or concerns as appropriate

9. *Parents:* Parents play critical roles in crisis management by
   - Following procedures established by school officials for responding in crisis situations, use of alternative sites, and other logistical requests
   - Learning to recognize children's psychological responses to crisis situations and being familiar with available school and community resources for dealing with these reactions
   - Supporting children and encouraging them to communicate their thoughts and concerns

- Avoiding finger-pointing and blame, focusing instead on healing and recovery as a first priority

- Being realistic as to what steps should be taken regarding security changes after a crisis incident

10. *Students:* Student roles in a crisis include

- Remaining as calm and quiet as possible

- Following the directions of adults

- Reporting any concerns or needs

These roles, along with additional roles for these and other positions, should be included in the crisis guidelines developed by school officials.

Transfer of Command

The school district crisis team offers support to building administrators, building crisis team members, and school staff. Although members of the building crisis team are truly the first crisis responders, some of the functions under their control are taken over by district-level crisis team members upon activation of that team and its guidelines. When public safety officials arrive, both building and district crisis teams yield most aspects of command to them, although command over general school issues remains with school administrators.

Public safety officials will, however, likely continue to look to school officials for ongoing input, because school officials are so familiar with students, staff, and some members of the broader community. School officials should, at a minimum, have the principal, custodian, and security official quickly available to brief public safety officials upon their arrival. Key players in the district incident response should also be available to public safety officials to ensure a smooth transfer of incident command management from the school to the public safety commanders.

Specific Considerations for Before, During, and After the Emergency Service Personnel Response

The exact steps school officials take in a crisis situation will depend largely on the exact circumstances of the particular crisis. Responses to the "What if?" situations referenced in Chapter 7 should provide district- and building-level crisis team members direction for processing specific types of incidents, providing that they have thoroughly processed these situations before an actual crisis. The roles and responsibilities identified in the preparatory stages will help guide school officials as to who should do what in various situations. Some important steps, however, are generally applicable to a number of different types of crises.

Before the Arrival of Emergency Services

Once an incident occurs and school officials contact police and other emergency service providers, they will need to continue their role as initial crisis response leaders until emergency personnel arrive. Evacuation, lockdown, or a combination of both is likely to occur during this time. Some suggested actions in this time period, when the circumstances warrant them, include

- Isolating the offender, weapon, and site of the incident
- Engaging lockdown and/or evacuation procedures
- Mobilizing school nurses and trained first responders to assist with medical needs until emergency medical services arrive
- Establishing necessary perimeters and preparing to direct traffic
- Having assigned crisis team members respond to the designated location to greet and escort first responders
- Securing the crime scene and overall building
- Remembering to secure, control, and communicate to all other students and staff not directly involved in the crisis, in addition to dealing with those directly involved
- Beginning to prepare for the *immediate* arrival of parents, followed shortly thereafter by the media, by engaging family reunification center operations and media liaison coordination
- Engaging other components of the "What if?" plan, including the role of the crisis team member responsible for documentation

Assisting Emergency Service Personnel

Once police, fire, medical, and/or other emergency service personnel arrive, it is important for school leaders to do the following:

- Make sure that school crisis team members and appropriate school leaders are clearly identifiable as decision makers in the school crisis, such as through the wearing of vests, hats, armbands, or other identifying clothing
- Ensure access for emergency service personnel to school grounds
- Assist emergency personnel in gaining direct access to those needing assistance
- Direct leaders from the school, school district, and emergency service agencies to an area designated as a command post or site for managing the incident, and ensure that the principal and/or assistant principal, custodian, and security representative are immediately available to emergency service personnel
- Designate a crisis team member or members to control access to the school and crime scene, and to escort legitimate officials to the appropriate areas
- Have the most recent student rosters, attendance and/or absentee lists, teacher absentee list, and teacher and substitute lists with emergency contacts and related information quickly available

- Be prepared for student and staff identification, especially when they are transported to the hospital

- Identify hospitals where the injured will be taken and identify who will be taken to which hospital; mobilize crisis team members to proceed to these same locations

- Engage accounting procedures for students and staff, if this has not already been done

- Engage parent notifications, if this has not already been done, beginning with the parents of those injured

After the Initial Emergency Service Responses

Once emergency personnel have responded to the site and the crisis response is beginning to stabilize, the work of the crisis team members is just beginning. Crisis officials will need to continue working, particularly in the following areas:

- School representatives at the hospital should be clearly identifiable, and should assist with victim identification and with coordination of parents and family, hospital security and staff, public information officials, and others. If possible, separate rooms should be set up for school officials, police officials, immediate family members, nonfamily visitors and guests, media, and others.

- Procedures for handling bloodborne pathogens should be followed within the parameters of not destroying crime scenes or interfering with police investigations.

- Crisis communications plans should be in full swing, including notifying parents, internal communications, and press briefings.

- Student debriefings should take place, as appropriate.

- A faculty meeting should be held to debrief and plan the next steps.

- Arrangements for counseling and mental health support should begin, including critical incident stress debriefing for crisis caregivers and others directly involved in the crisis.

- Consider scheduling a community meeting to discuss the crisis.

- Documentation efforts should be evaluated and continued.

- School legal counsel should be consulted and engaged as described in Chapter 9.

- Crisis team members should debrief at appropriate times to identify crisis response methods that worked and did not work during their management of the incident, and to modify their crisis preparedness guidelines accordingly.

As in other sections of this book, these are not exhaustive lists. Additional points will likely be raised in individual district and building crisis planning.

9

Preparing for the Post-Crisis Crisis

As if the preparation phases and actual management of the crisis situation were not enough, school and community officials need to realize that some of the most painful and stressful aspects of crisis management will continue after the initial incident itself has passed. In fact, this post-crisis crisis often seems just short of, if not sometimes worse than, the crisis incident itself in terms of length, intensity, and strain.

The four major areas affecting school and community leaders in their recovery from a crisis incident are

1. Crisis communications guidelines

2. Mental health support for grief and healing

3. Litigation preparedness

4. Financial considerations

It should be noted that these are not ranked in terms of their importance.

Crisis Communications Guidelines

Communications top the list as a constant theme for both those who have experienced school crises and those who have only experienced the planning for a crisis. Specific topics range from the physical side of communications (e.g., phones, public address systems, bullhorns, and so on) to the human side of communications (e.g., defining key audiences, dealing with the media, and related concerns). School officials should develop a set of very thorough crisis communications guidelines focusing on all aspects of communications far before an actual incident occurs.

Comprehensive Crisis Communications Guidelines

School officials often falsely believe that a crisis communications plan is something that lists who will speak with the media—or tells how to avoid speaking with the media! Although media relations is one element of a crisis communications plan, it is certainly not the only component. School officials must look at their internal communications with staff and students, as well as with significant others within the school community, such as parents, when developing comprehensive crisis communications guidelines.

Key Communications Functions

In a special publication to its members that shares the lessons learned from the Columbine tragedy, the National School Public Relations Association (NSPRA) presented a number of areas for structuring communications in a school crisis (Kaufman, Saltzman, Anderson, Carr, Pfeil, Armistead, & Kleinz, 1999). Their discussion included

- Leadership advisement to provide timely and accurate information and advice to the superintendent, board members, and administrative cabinet on issues, such as updates on criminal investigations, status of the injured, news briefing schedules and key messages, media coverage analysis, and special events
- Internal communication to all staff, employee groups, parents, and students on a daily basis through varied forms of message delivery (NSPRA emphasized that the internal communications function should be stressed over media responsiveness)
- External communication to key community leaders and communicators within the broader school community
- Media communications, including controlling the overwhelming amount of inquiries, researching inquiries, responding to inquiries, and monitoring media coverage
- Counseling communications coordination among psychologists, counselors, outside support agencies, and others
- Special events liaison to memorial services, political visitors, and other special activities
- Donations and volunteers communications to screen, organize, and respond to offers of donations and volunteer services
- Telephone bank coordination for hotlines, volunteer workers, updated fact sheets, and so forth
- Communications command center coordinator to assign tasks, disseminate messages, prepare parent letters, develop daily fact sheets for dissemination to staff and district communicators, update district

websites, send voice and e-mail messages to staff, and keep records of all communications

The article points out that a number of steps, such as structuring the communications plan, identifying roles and responsibilities, and related tasks, can and should be done before an actual crisis. For example, school officials may wish to seek donations and/or purchase communications command center equipment, such as fax machines, networked computers and phones, television sets, cell phones and batteries, and supplies, before they are needed. It would also be wise for local school officials to establish relationships with national associations, such as the NSPRA and their respective state chapters.

Media Relations Preparedness

The idea of the media knocking on a school administrator's door sends chills down the back of most school officials. The idea of multiple media representatives on the scene at one time turns the chills into a deep freeze. In a crisis situation, however, school officials can count on the media flocking to their doorsteps not only after the crisis, but perhaps even in the middle of the crisis itself!

Understanding Crisis Media Coverage Stages. As a school security supervisor and director, I learned a great deal about working with the media through trial and error. As a national consultant, I carried on my beliefs about the importance of understanding how the media works, what they need, and how to give it to them without hanging yourself and your organization in the process. This experience, along with having fielded well over 300 media interviews the month following the Columbine tragedy, has offered some helpful insights into the media handling of school crises.

There are at least seven identifiable stages of possible media coverage of a school crisis:

1. *Breaking News Stage.* This stage involves the first level of coverage as a crisis breaks, and will focus on getting information out to the public about the crisis as quickly as possible. There are generally few facts known at this stage, but the competition by the various media outlets to get the first facts is fierce.

2. *Investigation Stage.* Media representatives will shift from the breaking news stage quickly as soon as the investigation by police, school, and other officials is under way. Again, the focus at this stage is on securing as many details as possible about what exactly happened. Media representatives may also begin seeking information on how the crisis is affecting people and school operations, and may request access to buildings and students.

3. *Analysis Stage.* As the facts of the crisis begin to emerge, the media will attempt to provide an analysis, typically through "expert opinions," of exactly what occurred, why it occurred as it did, and what its impact on students, staff, and school operations will *really* mean. Because of media heli-

copters, the availability of 24-hours-a-day news programs, and other new technology, this stage may actually occur at the same time as stages one and two. In fact, it is not uncommon to see live news coverage of an unfolding school crisis at the same time that reporters make phone calls and attempt interviews to get details; and during all of this, there is an "expert" in the field being interviewed live from hundreds, if not thousands, of miles away from the actual crisis! It is also likely that part of the media analysis stage will focus on the impact of the school crisis on other schools in the community, other school districts, and so on, by asking, for example, how other school officials and students are reacting or what measures are in place at other schools to prevent such an incident.

4. *Grief Stage*. Here the media focus shifts to the impact of the crisis on the injured, their families, and/or the families and friends of deceased individuals. This stage of coverage may last a while, depending on the size and severity of the crisis, and will likely include coverage of funerals and memorials.

5. *Recovery and Return-to-Normal Stage*. Once funerals and memorials are over, the attention typically shifts to the recovery stage. The focus is then on how school officials, students, and the community are returning to normalcy.

6. *Future Predictions and Positive Angle Stage*. As schools and communities return to normal and the media exhausts its coverage of the grief and recovery stages, media outlets may seek to close their loop of coverage by focusing on what people can expect to occur in the future at the school crisis site or at other schools. The media may also take the approach of temporarily closing out coverage with a positive story about some aspect of the school or its operation.

7. *Anniversary Stage*. Depending on the nature of the crisis, the media may return to the crisis issue anywhere from one month to six months—or even one year—after the incident to acknowledge the anniversary of the crisis incident. The appearance of the media after wounds are starting to heal could simply reopen them. School officials need to note such dates on their calendar, and should anticipate return media coverage at that time.

Why School Officials Should Talk. School officials must recognize that by saying, "No comment," they are placing their reputation, and that of the school and district itself, in tremendous jeopardy. Reasons for talking to the media, especially at a time of crisis, include the following:

- If the media do not talk *with* you, they will talk *about* you.
- Talking with the media affords schools an opportunity to position themselves as being in charge and in control of the situation.
- The reputations and integrity of the school, the school district, and its leaders are at stake.
- The media provides the vehicle for school officials to reach their key audiences with timely and important messages.

No matter how much they dislike the media, educators must remember that if someone representing their school system does not communicate with the media, then the media will move on to other, and potentially less credible, sources who may be less familiar with the incident and the rationale behind the school response. School officials must be articulate, credible, decisive, confident, compassionate, empathetic, and clear not only in their actions while managing the crisis, but also in the messages they deliver during and after the crisis.

Managing the Media Madness. The NSPRA publication mentioned above best describes the impact of the media at a school crisis incident in its description of the Columbine High School crisis:

> Soon after the shooting began at Columbine High, more then 750 media outlets converged on Jeffco's [Jefferson County's] doorstep, creating a makeshift city that filled a nearby park. As Jeffco soon learned, the immediacy of today's media, with its global deadlines, around-the-clock coverage, and multiple communication channels creates nearly impossible demands. (Kaufman et al., 1999, p. 5)

Some tips provided by the NSPRA as a result of this experience include the following:

- Stick to your media policy once it is created.
- Identify spokespersons in advance, give them media training, and make sure that all staff know to refer media inquiries to the designated communications staff.
- Stress internal communications over media communications.
- "Triage" media inquiries, with priority going to local media over national and international media.
- Be prepared for the "new media," such as 24-hour news shows, online magazines, chat rooms, and other new technology media.
- Control media access, as appropriate, and include regularly scheduled news briefings and use of media pools when necessary.
- Develop key messages, stick to them, and ensure that the communications team works with the legal team.

Other Media Preparedness Tips. Some additional preparation tips include the following:

1. Create and maintain an updated emergency contact list of key communicators with names and phone numbers. I recommend that a database with names, phone numbers, fax numbers, and e-mail addresses be established and, if at all possible, that a broadcast group be created on fax machines, e-mail, and at least internally on voice mail so that messages can be sent quickly and easily if a crisis creates a need for mass messaging.

2. Create a fact sheet for the district and for each school with the school name, address, and phone number; administrators' names; the number of students and staff, along with related demographics; grade levels; building details, including the age of the school and number of classrooms; and information on any special programs or achievements.

3. Determine who will be spokesperson ahead of time, use that person consistently, and, if at all possible, avoid having board members, the superintendent, or the principal as the lead spokesperson, because they will be needed more to manage the crisis and the recovery than to stay in front of the media all day, for weeks on end. In addition, make sure that the school spokesperson works closely with the public information officers from police and other emergency service agencies.

4. Respond quickly and early with available facts, and provide even just a few facts as soon as you know them.

5. Hold press conferences away from the scene of the tragedy.

6. Answer those questions that you can, but do not speculate and do not hesitate to explain why you cannot answer a question.

7. View your comments from the eyes of the public, and remember to include compassion and depth in your answers.

8. Remind reporters of the need for privacy and healing, and take steps to return the school to normalcy.

9. Be able to articulate steps taken to make schools safe, to reduce security risks, and to prepare for effectively managing crisis situations, and discuss how school staff followed the guidelines in place to best handle the situation.

10. Know your audience, prepare for interviews and press conferences, develop and communicate your key messages, make sure that everyone being interviewed is on the same page, and remember that good public and media relations is not "spin," but involves effectively communicating good practices and behavior, which must be in place before—and during—the crisis.

Lessons for the Media on Covering Ongoing Crises

The Poynter Institute for Media Studies (Steele, 1999) offers the following guidelines for media representatives covering an ongoing crisis situation:

- Assume that the offender(s) have access to the reporting.
- Avoid reporting and showing information that could jeopardize the safety of law enforcement and other public safety officials, including keeping news helicopters away from the area and not reporting information heard over police scanners.
- Notify authorities if the suspect contacts the newsroom, and do not attempt to contact or interview the suspect during the incident.

- Avoid giving comments or analysis of the demands being made by the suspect during the incident.
- Be cautious when interviewing family members and friends so that the interview does not serve as a vehicle for the suspect and his or her family to communicate with each other.

In another publication, the Poynter Institute recommends a number of ethical questions for reporters to ask themselves prior to their coverage of school-related bomb threats (Tompkins, 1999). These questions focus on journalistic duties, story impact, potential consequences of coverage, tone and words used in the coverage, and covering the overall process more than the actual events. Media management and reporters should discuss and plan for dealing with school and other crisis incidents ahead of time, just as school officials should plan for the prevention and management of an actual crisis.

Mental Health Support for Grief and Healing

The crisis preparedness perspectives in this book are primarily from a professional school security perspective, not from that of a school psychologist or other mental health professional. In fact, there are a number of valuable resources, including those listed in the Recommended Resources section of this book, that address school crisis management entirely from the perspectives of psychologists and counselors. Clearly, the security, tactical, and related public safety perspectives must be balanced with caring, compassion, and an intense amount of mental health support for students, staff, parents, and the overall community affected by a school crisis.

Experts from *School Crisis Response: A CISM Perspective* (Johnson, Casey, Ertl, Everly, & Mitchell, 1999) note that the entire mission of educational organizations is compromised by post-traumatic stress in a variety of ways:

- Children reexperience traumatic events to integrate them into their understanding of the world and, in doing so, create adverse reactions that affect learning.
- Heightened physiological arousal results from the traumatic images and reduces the ability of children to concentrate.
- Any distractions cause a startle reflex, which disrupts attention.
- Children react to trauma by regressing to earlier levels of coping. Children also integrate reenactments of the trauma into play with others, which in turn interferes with socialization.
- Difficulties occur in memory retention and retrieval.
- Children become disassociated.
- Disassociation, attention and concentration difficulties, and associated behaviors can be misread by staff as discipline issues.
- Preoccupation with the traumatic experience detracts from a child's ability to benefit fully from school experiences.

Furthermore, Steele (1998) identifies four possible avenues of exposure to both acute stress reactions and posttraumatic stress disorder (PTSD) reactions:

1. As a surviving victim

2. As a witness to a potential trauma-inducing incident

3. Being related to the victim or victims

4. Verbal exposure to the details of traumatic experiences

Considering the potential for children to be exposed to traumatic incidents, and knowing the impact such exposure has on educational settings, mental health issues stemming from school crises clearly must be addressed in a timely and effective manner if educators expect children to gain the most from the classroom.

Johnson (1993) notes,

> Reactions to loss can be a part of other crises or they can be the primary focus of the crisis experience. . . . Most people, including children, react to loss in a stereotypical pattern. . . . Most theories hold a core pattern similar to that presented by Elizabeth Kübler-Ross, who, in her book *On death and dying*, puts forth a five-step process of denial, anger, bargaining, depression, and acceptance. Other theories include stages of guilt, fear of the future, sadness, and renewal. (p. 102)

Children and adults must therefore understand that when grieving, they are experiencing normal reactions to abnormal situations. The ability of students and adults to negotiate through these or similar stages, and the amount of time they need to do so, will depend on the severity of the crisis, the individual's understanding of the incident, the support system of the grieving person, and other factors unique to the individual and to the incident. It is important that officials experiencing a school crisis work with mental health specialists to provide services to help both students and staff through the normal grieving process and, if necessary, to facilitate further support for those who experience more adverse reactions.

Poland and McCormick (1999) offer detailed suggestions for what schools can do in the aftermath of a school crisis to help students and staff effectively undergo the grief and healing processes. These include

- Reopening school as soon as possible, especially to reduce the chance of "school phobia" occurring
- Avoiding significant alterations of the school environment before students return
- Adequately preparing teachers and staff for the return of students, and ensuring that they carefully plan for their students' return
- Continuing to provide emotional assistance to students and staying in contact with parents

- Providing structure in the days after the crisis, but being flexible enough to modify the curriculum to address the crisis, such as by incorporating artwork, drama skits, music, poems and other writing exercises, and memorial efforts into classroom and school activities

Poland and McCormick also provide extensive suggestions for parents, the community, and the caregivers that should be addressed before expectations of a return to normalcy can be seriously considered. Educators should receive staff in-service training designed to familiarize them with the management of stress from critical incidents, the grief and healing process, and related mental health issues and resources.

School officials should be aware of national and state resources available to help with the mental health component of school crisis recovery. The National Organization for Victim Assistance and the National Association of School Psychologists both have response teams that can provide on-site mental health support in processing school crises and moving forward with school and community recovery efforts. Educators would also be wise to identify all local, regional, and state resources that can be tapped into in the event of a major crisis incident in their district.

Litigation Preparedness

Unfortunately, we live in a litigious society. It is not a matter of *if* you will be sued, but rather of *when* you will be sued, especially following a school crisis incident.

Legal counsel should be involved in the complete crisis preparedness process. In the preparation stages, counsel should have input into, and review of, crisis guidelines. In the post-crisis crisis stage, counsel should be involved in the following processes:

- Review of documentation development
- Review of public information dissemination procedures and content
- Liaison with prosecutors for criminal charges, as appropriate

It is likely that, in addition to school attorneys, school leaders will also work hand-in-hand with not only school risk managers, but also insurance representatives, as insurance claims and related issues will likely be raised for an extended period of time following the crisis.

School officials must remember that, as difficult as it is to do, they must make every effort to document details of their response to crisis situations. Ideally, school officials should also have ample evidence of the many steps taken before an incident to reduce the risks and to prepare for managing a crisis. Although litigation concerns are legitimate, those concerns must also be balanced with caring and compassion in responding to the crisis aftermath.

Financial Considerations

The costs associated with recovery from a crisis incident can be tremendous. Although costs associated with a horrific incident could range into the millions, even a smaller-scale crisis, such as an ongoing demonstration or protest, can cost thousands or even hundreds of thousands in overtime, physical plant management, and other operations expenses. Some of the specific cost areas associated with a crisis recovery can include

- Manpower and associated overtime costs for those managing the crisis
- Physical plant operations for extended hours
- Repairs and replacement of damaged or stolen property
- Support services, such as additional mental health and related counseling services, or security and policing services

Officials responsible for school budget management and business services should develop a disaster recovery plan that includes a mechanism for accounting for crisis-related costs, and should do so before any actual incident so that, if a crisis occurs, they will have a structure in place from which to work.

State and Federal Support Strategies

There are many steps that local schools, law enforcement agencies, and safe schools stakeholders can, and should, take to reduce risks and to prepare for managing school crises. Although such efforts largely fall to local, county, and regional officials, there are steps that state and federal officials should take to support local efforts.

Chapter 10 highlights the ongoing initiatives of state leaders in Indiana to support local safe schools efforts. Chapter 11 closes this book with a look at how all states, as well as the federal government and other entities, can provide support to local schools nationwide.

10

Indiana

An Example of Leadership in State and Local Preparedness

Leadership is the number one requirement when it comes to having meaningful safe schools efforts. This is true not only at the local level, but also for those state and federal organizations providing support to local schools.

In over 15 years of working in the school security field, I have personally witnessed more than my share of school politics. In fact, I unquestionably hold that politics has been the number one obstacle to schools having meaningful security and crisis preparedness measures in place up until the spate of school shootings in the late 1990s. This perspective is probably my primary bias, and so a great deal of work and sincerity must be present for me to be truly impressed by any large organizations, especially government agencies.

State leaders in Indiana have consistently earned my trust and respect for their leadership in safe schools efforts, particularly in their support of balancing prevention and intervention efforts with security and crisis preparedness measures. State Superintendent Suellen Reed has lead the Indiana Department of Education to a position warranting national recognition for its leadership in supporting school safety, security, and crisis preparedness initiatives. The department's Office of Student Services, under the direction of Steve Davis and with the diligence of school safety specialist Cathy Danyluk, has developed the respect and support of local school officials throughout Indiana for their ongoing programmatic and financial support of the safe schools initiatives described below.

Indiana Governor Frank O'Bannon has also demonstrated leadership in placing school safety at the top of the state's agenda. Governor O'Bannon and his education aide, Larry Grau, have worked hard to create and maintain legislative support, and have expanded funding for school safety training and programmatic support throughout Indiana. Their unwavering commitment to school safety has been illustrated in their push to establish and build upon numerous safe schools initiatives.

One of the most interesting dynamics has been the bipartisan manner in which both Dr. Reed and Governor O'Bannon, members of rival political parties, have set aside party politics to ensure progress on school safety measures. Many times, across the nation, we hear elected officials *talking* about the need for a bipartisan focus on school safety; in Indiana, I have witnessed them not only "talking the talk," but more importantly "walking the walk."

Indiana's Safe Schools History

In a memorandum to me in June 1999, Cathy Danyluk summarized Indiana's safe schools history. The Indiana Department of Education's Office of Student Services provides technical assistance and consultation to school districts in the areas of emergency preparedness and crisis intervention. The DOE's working definitions include *emergency preparedness*, referring to policies, procedures, and programs that a school establishes to prevent harm to people or school property; and *crisis intervention*, meaning the policies, procedures, and programs that a school offers to the school community in the aftermath of an emergency (i.e., a crisis).

An overview of the office's history in dealing with these areas, in addition to their other programs on safe and drug-free schools, was provided in Danyluk's memo and is highlighted below to illustrate how a state-level agency can, indeed, provide ongoing support to local districts in the listed areas.

Capacity Building for Crisis Intervention

1987: Crisis intervention was the single topic of the Indiana Department of Education, Office of Student Services' Summer Institute. Also that year, the *Suicide and Crisis Intervention Guide* was written in cooperation with the Indiana Department of Health and sent to school corporations.

1991: The Indiana Student Services Summer Institute focused on school and community collaboration around child and adolescent mental health issues, with crisis intervention being highlighted.

1995: The *Indiana Suicide and Crisis Intervention Guide* was updated and sent to all school corporations, and three workshops featuring the guide were held.

1998: The *Indiana School Health Manual* and *Student Assistance Manual,* published in 1998, both have crisis intervention sections. That year, six conflict mediation workshops were sponsored by the Indiana Department of Education, Office of Student Services, and assistance was provided to Project PEACE (Peaceful Endings through Attorneys, Children, and Educators), a conflict mediation program offered through the Indiana Attorney General's Office and the Indiana State Board Association. This assistance will continue annually. Also that year, the Indiana State Board of Education rule 511 I.A.C. §4-1.5-7, effective July 1, 2000, was created and requires school corporations to develop a crisis intervention plan in concert with the emergency preparedness plan required under 511 I.A.C. §6.1-2-2.5.

Capacity Building for Emergency Preparedness

1987: An advisory group on safe schools (the Marion County School Violence Prevention Committee) was formed.

1994: The *Safe School Guide* was written by the advisory group, and five regional workshops were held.

1995: Three regional workshops on gangs and school safety were conducted. An Indiana School Safety Leadership Consortium was appointed by Dr. Reed, and all consortium members received school safety leadership training from the National School Safety Center.

1996: State assistance was provided in the production of a school crisis video.

1997: Two regional workshops were presented that year by the authors of a safe schools handbook commissioned by the National Association of Secondary School Principals. Also in 1997, Clay Community Schools were awarded a grant to develop a model crisis intervention/emergency preparedness plan for rural schools.

1998: Four regional workshops on emergency preparedness, featuring Kenneth Trump, President of National School Safety and Security Services, and members of the Indiana School Safety Leadership Consortium, were held. That year, the Indiana State Board of Education also promulgated Rule 511 I.A.C. §6.1-2-2.5 (Safe Schools and Emergency Preparedness Planning). The rule requires all school corporations, in consultation with local public safety agencies, to develop a written emergency plan for natural as well as manmade disasters (student disturbance, weapon, weapon of mass destruction, contamination of water or air supply, hostage, and kidnapping incidents).

Furthermore, in 1998 the Marion County School Violence Prevention Committee worked with Indiana Attorney General Jeff Modisett on the *School Search Manual*, which was distributed to all school corporations and law enforcement agencies. In addition, nine regional workshops were conducted by members of the Safe Schools Leadership Consortium to assist school districts in the development of their emergency plans. Each district received a copy of a school crisis video and a school security book, in addition to handout materials and presentations.

1999: The Indiana Department of Education's *Checklist for a Safe and Secure School Environment* was completed and distributed to all school corporations and law enforcement agencies. (See Resource B for the checklist.)

In addition to federal legislation for safe and drug-free schools, Indiana passed firearm and dangerous weapon expulsion legislation and created a fund for safe schools needs in 1995. By 1997, the Safe Haven Program had provided more than $3 million to schools for safety and violence prevention programs.

In 1998 and 1999, Governor O'Bannon initiated and supported the amendment of the Safe Haven Program as Indiana's Safe Schools Fund. Under the revised legislation, $3 million will be awarded to schools for Safe Haven, emergency preparedness, or school safety programs. The legislature also appropriated $750,000 annually, consistent with Governor O'Bannon's proposal, for use in providing training to one school safety specialist from each school district across the state. Additionally, $2,000 was appropriated for each school corporation to use for participation in county school safety commissions projects for developing local crisis and safety guidelines.

As a result of this legislation, the Indiana School Safety Specialist Academy was created to provide a 40-hour annual training program to one school safety specialist from each school district in Indiana. The academy program, currently in its first year and coordinated by Clarissa Snapp, is operated by the Indiana Department of Education. First-year curriculum strands include topics focused on best practices in school safety, comprehensive safe schools planning, legal and policy issues, violence prevention and school crisis management, and school-community partnerships.

Local Safe Schools Leadership

A number of local school districts in Indiana have exerted leadership in school security and crisis preparedness areas. Working methodically to strengthen security and crisis preparedness measures while still respecting and supporting the need for prevention, intervention, and other climate-related programs have been the Indianapolis Public Schools, under the direction of school police chief Jack Martin; the Lawrence Township Metropolitan School District in Indianapolis, under the direction of Dr. Duane Hodgin, Assistant Superintendent; the Wayne Township Metropolitan School District, led by its coordinator of security, Chuck Hibbert; Pike Township Metropolitan School District, led by school police chief Al Kasper; and the Fort Wayne Community School District, under the guidance of security coordinator John Weicker. I have also had the good fortune to work with school officials in Hammond, Highland, Marion, and too many other districts throughout Indiana to list, all of them demonstrating that with the proper leadership, state and local officials can marshal resources and work collaboratively in the best interests of improving all components of a comprehensive safe schools plan.

My focus on Indiana certainly should not lead readers to believe that Indiana is the only state in the nation working on school safety. Illinois state officials, too, have provided extensive resources to local districts through statewide regional training programs and technical assistance sessions, and a number of other states have created or intensified their safe schools efforts, especially following the high profile incidents of the late 1990s. Some states, however, still lag behind the times, especially when it comes to balancing their prevention and intervention support with school security and crisis preparedness focuses.

The progress by Indiana officials, however, highlights the importance of a number of factors required for states successfully to provide meaningful support to local schools. These include

- A politically bipartisan approach to school safety
- A balance of prevention and intervention with security and crisis preparedness measures
- Dedicated dollars to help districts meet mandates and suggested practices
- Allowing input into legislation, policy making, and programs from people with specialized knowledge and frontline experience in school safety
- Demonstrating that successful state-level support of local districts requires a commitment to the ongoing process of school safety, and not seeing safety as a one-time (and often politically driven) event

Specific school safety strategies that state officials can take are highlighted in Chapter 11.

11

Where Do We Go From Here?

Many local school officials on the front lines are aggressively seeking steps to improve the security in the here-and-now at their schools. State and federal agencies, along with private and nonprofit professional organizations, must step up to the plate and deliver on the security and crisis preparedness components, just as they have in years past on prevention and intervention programs geared toward school safety. There are many simple, cost-effective, and practical things that can be done in ways that are meaningful and helpful to local schools.

In the midst of the several high-profile school shootings that captured the nation's attention during the late 1990s, I heard many state officials across the nation indicate that there is nothing states can do to help prevent or manage such crises. I recall getting that gut-wrenching feeling in my stomach when these comments were made, because I know that state officials can take—and should have taken—some affirmative steps to help local school districts. The federal government, colleges of education, and academic researchers need to join the states in balancing their commitments to school safety, moving away from a strict intervention and prevention approach toward one that mixes these with reasonable security and crisis preparedness measures.

State-Level Strategies

There are many things that state governments can do to improve school security and crisis preparedness. For example, they can

- Improve school crime reporting requirements to ensure that crimes are consistently reported both to law enforcement and to a centralized state data collection site (states should provide training and technical assistance to school officials on crime reporting, and the failure to adhere to crime reporting requirements should be enforced with specific sanctions)

- Provide a legal foundation for law enforcement officials to notify schools of student crimes in the community
- Require safe schools plans and crisis preparedness guidelines, and enforce such requirements with specific sanctions for those who fail to adhere
- Provide resources for enhanced and ongoing security-related staffing, while recognizing that different districts may employ different models, such as school resource officers, in-house school security staff, or school police departments
- Provide state-certified training for school security and police personnel, and, if possible, for other school safety representatives
- Obtain ongoing, direct input from school security and school policing officials into legislative and other hearings related to safe schools
- Provide security-specific funds, such as grant pools, for security and crisis training and planning; school security assessments by qualified professionals; equipment, including such items as communications equipment and cameras; anonymous reporting mechanisms, such as hotlines; and crime data collection, analysis, and reporting tools
- Enhance penalties for school crimes, such as assault of school personnel or weapons possession (of all types, not only firearms)
- Improve education requirements for educators in undergraduate and graduate schools by requiring or providing incentives for college education programs to include safe schools courses, and by supporting professional organizations that focus on security and crisis preparedness and training for school support staff, such as bus drivers, secretaries, and custodians
- Create education programs for law enforcement officials within police academies and in special programs dealing with school safety
- Target education decision makers, such as boards, superintendents, and principals, for educational programs and resources designed to better prepare them for dealing with school security and crisis preparedness
- Balance security and crisis preparedness initiatives with prevention and intervention program support
- Strengthen prevention and intervention programs, such as alternative schools and programs (even for the elementary level), resources for special education students, mental health and psychological services, conflict management and social skills, and classroom management and crisis skills
- Consider establishing a centralized school safety center that will serve as the lead state agency and clearinghouse on school safety, providing training and technical support, publishing reports and re-

source materials, and increasing public awareness of school security and crisis preparedness issues; such a center should focus on trends and issues, research and best practices, prevention and intervention strategies, security and crisis preparedness measures, and overall safe schools planning

This list should help guide those who believe that there is nothing that states can do to prevent and manage school crises.

The Federal Role

Federal government officials have improved their efforts to address the security and crisis preparedness components of school safety in recent years. Although past efforts have typically focused on the prevention and intervention components, gradual steps are being taken toward opening the door to security and crisis preparedness through additional funding support for school resource officer programs, a closer examination of the use of technology, and more willingness to utilize at least some federal funds for other security and crisis preparedness measures. Federal officials need to stop arguing over whether to provide more prevention *or* tighter security, and should instead concentrate their efforts on providing more prevention *and* tighter security. They also need to recognize that a professional school security program does not automatically equate to simply more manpower and more equipment in our schools. Federal funding of school security and crisis programs should follow along the lines of the state-level recommendations presented in the previous section.

Colleges of Education

Colleges providing teacher and administrator programs need to take a leadership role in better preparing school officials on school safety and crisis preparedness issues. The most common response heard when this issue has been raised is that there is not enough time (or money) in the college curriculum for additional required courses. At best, then, programs on school safety issues are incorporated as a short segment in other courses or as an elective or special topic.

It is logical to believe that at least one reason for the difficulty in recruiting and retaining teachers centers on issues of discipline and workplace safety for both students and staff. To toss new teachers into environments for which they have not been adequately prepared and then to expect them to perform effectively and remain on the job is unrealistic. The first line of defense in reducing school violence is a well-prepared school employee, and colleges must recognize and respond to this need for well-prepared school employees by requiring or providing a unit on school safety in their curricula.

The Academic Dilemma

A number of academicians have been quick to discard school security and crisis preparedness on the basis that, as they say, "there is no research to support that these measures work." Ironically, the reason that there is no research on the effectiveness of security and crisis preparedness strategies is because there have been no researchers interested in or able (i.e., funded) to conduct this type of research. In fact, there has been little effective communication over the years between the prevention and intervention communities typically associated with academic researchers and the security and crisis preparedness world *not* associated with academic researchers.

Education, prevention, and intervention programs cannot be delivered with maximum effectiveness in unsafe settings, and a balanced and rational security and crisis preparedness program is necessary for safe educational settings to exist. Yet the absence of research on and evaluation of such programs has led to us having no data, and therefore to there being no formal recognition of school security and crisis preparedness as a professional discipline within the school community. This has, in turn, led to scarce resources and little credibility for the school security perspective (at least until the school shootings of the late 1990s occurred) and, ultimately, to slow progress on improving security and crisis preparedness in our schools.

Ironically, some of these academicians, many of them never having worked on school safety issues in K-12 schools, are using the absence of research as justification for advocating that we not consider implementing school security and crisis preparedness measures. One need only look at the years of research and evaluation conducted on prevention and intervention programs to find countless conclusions that many of these programs were not working successfully, yet the academic world readily encourages the funding and support of more prevention programs, not to mention more new research and evaluation of prevention and intervention programs.

One could therefore easily argue that those academicians quick to shoot down security and crisis preparedness strategies based on a lack of research should then logically also be against prevention and intervention programs, because many of these programs have been found in evaluation and research to be unsuccessful or questionable. It would certainly be ludicrous to suggest that prevention and intervention programs should be eliminated based simply on past research findings, and it is equally ludicrous to suggest that we ignore basic security and crisis strategies simply because there is no research on the subject.

In short, the "absence of research" argument is old, misused, and irrelevant in the big picture of things—especially in the eyes of victims of school violence and their families, both of whom are looking for answers on how to secure schools right now. Nevertheless, one academician at a national conference on school safety asked me if I was aware of any research that indicated that reducing the number of open doors could prevent someone from getting inside a school! Common sense should tell us that such steps as reducing the number of open doors, greeting visitors, reporting strangers, locking doors to high-value storage areas, preparing for natural and man-made disasters, and other security and crisis measures are all prudent measures to take in today's society and at our schools.

This is not to say that there should never be any research and evaluation on school security and crisis preparedness components. In fact, it would be quite appropriate to research and evaluate the roles and effectiveness of

- School security and school policing staffing models
- Security equipment and technology in schools
- Crisis planning and training strategies
- Security assessments and planning focused on physical security, crime prevention, and other measures
- School-police-community partnerships
- Specific security-related strategies, such as use of drug sniffing dogs, hotlines, or uniforms

However, those researchers who have no interest in studying these areas should, at a minimum, stop using the absence of research as justification for not supporting security and crisis programs. Because these individuals have yet to perfect the prevention and intervention fields, they should be less critical (especially with no supporting evidence) of the security and crisis preparedness fields.

Other Players

School safety is a broad concept with many components. School officials alone cannot be left the job of providing safe schools. Parents, students, public safety agencies, elected officials, residents, and many others must play an active and productive role in the process, and the process must be ongoing.

Where To Now?

The Columbine High School tragedy has taken school safety to a new level in the minds of educators. In doing so, it has caused many to realize finally that balanced and rational school security and crisis preparedness strategies are warranted, provided that they are reasonable in scope and nature. This book serves as a tool to help school and public safety officials remain balanced and focused as they develop their crisis preparedness processes. We can only hope that everyone will use these guidelines and related processes for their preparation for crises—and that no one will ever have a real-life school crisis for which they will have to put all of this preparation to the test.

Resource A

Critical Questions in Hiring a School Security Consultant

Answers to these and related questions should provide school officials with a better awareness of the potential capabilities and motives of consultants seeking to do business with their districts. Of course, references and backgrounds should always be thoroughly checked before hiring any consultant.

1. Was the consultant in business to provide school security-specific services on a regular, ongoing basis before the high-profile school violence tragedies of the late 1990s?

2. Is the consultant affiliated with a product?

3. Does the consultant have a long-term history of working firsthand with violent and delinquent children? In particular, was this a position of full-time responsibility for school security and crisis issues in K-12 school settings? Is the consultant now twisting work experience in a remotely related area into a proclaimed expertise in school security?

4. Is this the consultant's primary, full-time employment, or is this a part-time income, post-retirement job, or new market expansion by a company whose primary expertise is in other areas?

5. Does the consultant's perspective come primarily from an academic or theoretical perspective, or has he or she actually worked in K-12 schools—and worked specifically with violent youth and school safety issues?

6. Is your school district being used as a "guinea pig" so that the consultant can build a client list of school districts? (Is this perhaps why some "experts" are offering their school safety expertise and services for free?)

7. Does the consultant and his or her company have a well-established, long-term reputation? Do their peers in the school safety field recognize them, and are they recognized as being indepen- dent, credible, and on the cutting edge in the field?

8. Does the consulting firm have a history primarily in a peripherally related area of service, such as in providing security guards or private detective investigations, military security, or law enforcement, or is it in K-12 school security?

9. Is the consultant or his or her firm hiding behind titles like *"non-profit" organization* or *"research" foundation,* or other institutional or organizational names when, in essence, they are primarily for-profit consultants?

10. Is the consulting firm a larger, more generalized company seeking to "widgetize" the school security industry by packaging and mass-producing generic, canned programs and services for sale to many schools for the purpose of broadening their income base?

Resource B

Indiana Department of Education Checklist for a Safe and Secure School Environment

In June of 1999, the Indiana Department of Education published the *Checklist for a Safe and Secure School Environment* as "a means of evaluating not only existing emergency plans but also the other essential ingredients of a comprehensive school safety program," according to Dr. Suellen Reed, Superintendent of Public Instruction (Reed, 1999, p. 3). The checklist is one of numerous resources provided by the department to Indiana schools. This list, along with more detailed information and resources, is available on the department's website at *www.doe.state.in.us*.

Contributors to the *Checklist for a Safe and Secure School Environment* include

- Steve Davis, Phyllis Lewis, Kevin McDowell, and Kimb Stewart of the Indiana Department of Education
- Tanya Douglas and Jack Martin of the Indianapolis Public Schools
- Duane Hodgin of the Lawrence Township Metropolitan School District
- Joseph Wainscott of the Indiana State Police

Leah Ingraham of Marian College served as the project editor, and a number of individuals also served as reviewers.

Checklist for a Safe and Secure School Environment

Name of School _____

Principal _____

Checklist Item	Activity	Responsible Person(s)	Month of Safety Planning												
			1	2	3	4	5	6	7	8	9	10	11	12
1. Philosophy, Mission and School Climate	**1.1** Review mission for "secure environment" emphasis													
	1.2 Conduct school climate survey													
	1.3 Screen staff													
2. Partnerships with Community and Parents	**2.1** Identify community resources													
	2.2 Include student leaders													
	2.3 Secure parent support													
	2.4 Form "Safe School Working Group"													
3. Safety Policy, Procedures, Plans	**3.1** Review existing policy-procedure and plan(s)													
	3.2 Identify gaps or weaknesses													
	3.3 Link to county emergency plan													
	3.4 Plan for medical emergencies													
	3.5 Develop media relationships													
	3.6 Assign school staff roles													
	3.7 Arrange trainings for staff and students													
	3.8 Conduct table-top exercises													
	3.9 Communicate policy-procedures to parents													

SOURCE: Indiana Department of Education. (1999.) *Checklist for a Safe and Secure School Environment*. Authorized for use as stipulated by the Indiana Department of Education.

Trump, K. *Classroom Killers? Hallway Hostages? How Schools Can Prevent and Manage School Crises*. © 2000. Corwin Press, Inc.

Checklist for a Safe and Secure School Environment

Name of School _____

Principal _____

Checklist Item	Activity	Responsible Person(s)	Month of Safety Planning											
			1	2	3	4	5	6	7	8	9	10	11	12
4. Arrangements for School Security Staff	4.1 Review current security staffing													
	4.2 Add security staff or links to law enforcement if needed													
	4.3 Offer trainings for security staff													
5. Student Conduct in the School Setting	5.1 Review disciplinary policies for consistency and updates													
	5.2 Distinguish between criminal and misconduct offenses													
	5.3 Reinstate students with misconduct offenses													
	5.4 Consider restorative justice													
	5.5 Report criminal activity to authorities													
	5.6 Survey teachers for classroom management needs													
	5.7 Review current directives on discipline in special education													
6. Curriculum	6.1 Review health and social skills lessons for support of school safety													
	6.2 Give instruction in anger control conflict management, and reasoned decision-making													

SOURCE: Indiana Department of Education. (1999.) *Checklist for a Safe and Secure School Environment.* Authorized for use as stipulated by the Indiana Department of Education.

Trump, K. *Classroom Killers? Hallway Hostages? How Schools Can Prevent and Manage School Crises.* © 2000. Corwin Press, Inc.

Checklist for a Safe and Secure School Environment

Name of School _____

Principal _____

Checklist Item	Activity	Responsible Person(s)	Month of Safety Planning											
			1	2	3	4	5	6	7	8	9	10	11	12
7. Student Support	7.1 Roles for advisory program													
	7.2 Role for student assistance, counseling, and referral													
	7.3 Make early referrals for troubled students													
	7.4 Evaluate peer programs for role in school safety													
	7.5 Review after-school programs													
	7.6 Consider a hotline for tips on potential safety problems													
	7.7 Follow-up on all rumors													
8. Drugs and Gang Prevention/ Intervention	8.1 Arrange updates and information exchange with authorities													
	8.2 Review dress code with respect to gang "colors", etc.													
	8.3 Arrange updates on drugs and gangs for school staff and parents													
	8.4 Update and revise drug education curriculum as needed													
	8.5 Review search procedures													
	8.6 Monitor, record, report and remove gang related graffiti													

SOURCE: Indiana Department of Education. (1999.) *Checklist for a Safe and Secure School Environment*. Authorized for use as stipulated by the Indiana Department of Education.

Trump, K. *Classroom Killers? Hallway Hostages? How Schools Can Prevent and Manage School Crises*. © 2000. Corwin Press, Inc.

Checklist for a Safe and Secure School Environment

Name of School _____

Principal _____

Checklist Item	Activity	Responsible Person(s)	Month of Safety Planning											
			1	2	3	4	5	6	7	8	9	10	11	12
9. Assess Buildings and Grounds for Safety	9.1 Control all entrances and exits													
	9.2 Review keying and locks													
	9.3 Assess and remove obstacles preventing observation of grounds													
	9.4 Acknowledge all school visitors													
	9.5 Arrange effective communication within the school and to the outside													
	9.6 Examine exterior/interior lighting for safety													
	9.7 Provide blueprints/maps of building and grounds to police, and fire department													
10. Violence Prevention at Competitive Sports Events	10.1 Develop event specific strategies													
	10.2 Promote sportsmanship													
	10.3 Encourage positive pep club activities													
	10.4 Arrange event staffing and procedures													

SOURCE: Indiana Department of Education. (1999.) *Checklist for a Safe and Secure School Environment*. Authorized for use as stipulated by the Indiana Department of Education.

Trump, K. *Classroom Killers? Hallway Hostages? How Schools Can Prevent and Manage School Crises.* © 2000. Corwin Press, Inc.

Checklist for a Safe and Secure School Environment

Name of School _____

Principal _____

Checklist Item	Activity	Responsible Person(s)	Month of Safety Planning											
			1	2	3	4	5	6	7	8	9	10	11	12
11. Transportation Needs for Safety Planning	11.1 Acquaint parents and students with school bus conduct rules													
	11.2 Provide training for evacuations													
	11.3 Arrange pick-up/drop-off locations for evacuations													
	11.4 Set field trip procedures													
12. Records and Evaluation	12.1 Define and record "safety incidents"													
	12.2 Report criminal activity to proper authorities													
	12.3 Review incident data and update staff													
	12.4 Debrief after "incidents"													
	12.5 Conduct on-going formative evaluation													

SOURCE: Indiana Department of Education. (1999.) *Checklist for a Safe and Secure School Environment.* Authorized for use as stipulated by the Indiana Department of Education.

Trump, K. *Classroom Killers? Hallway Hostages? How Schools Can Prevent and Manage School Crises.* © 2000. Corwin Press, Inc.

154

Resource C

Sample "What If?" Scenarios

Chapter 7 discussed the use of "What If?" scenarios in helping crisis team members create effective crisis guidelines. Some sample scenarios are listed below to illustrate that they need not be lengthy, difficult, or complex. Scenarios do, however, need to be realistic and able to generate brainstorming by crisis team members.

In each scenario, crisis team members should ask themselves the following questions:

- What issues would we need to address and what actions would we need to take to address the immediate problem and subsequent related issues?
- What preparations can we make to prevent such an incident from happening or, if one has already occurred, how might we better manage a repeat of such an incident?

Sample Scenarios

Scenario One: A Large Altercation

It is five minutes into the Monday opening of your high school or middle school day. As students enter the school, a large altercation starts on the second-floor back hallway, the location of several fights in the past involving students from rival groups in your school. The participants include at least 20 active fighters, and a crowd of hundreds begins filling the hallways, where several spin-off fights occur. At least one staff member and numerous students are injured. As this is occurring, parents who were dropping off their children outside enter the building to see what is happening. Calls begin pouring in to the main office about 10 minutes after the start of the disruption, including several calls from the media.

Scenario Two: A Bus Accident

It is 20 minutes after school dismissal at your elementary school. You are in the office when you receive a phone call from a local radio reporter, who tells you that a school bus carrying 38 of your students and two adults (including the driver) was involved in an accident while returning to your school from a field trip. The accident, involving a semitrailer and another school bus, is believed to involve injuries.

Scenario Three: Shots Fired

You work in a school where all of the doors are secured from the outside except the main entrance. There are 20 surveillance cameras strategically positioned throughout the building, and several security personnel patrol the campus. At 11:15 a.m., during a lunch period, a male teenager enters the building through a side door, walks through the building to the school cafeteria, and stops about 15 feet from the assistant principal. He then pulls out a gun, points toward a group of seated students, and fires one round, hitting the wall but missing the students. He then flees the building. Three television stations and 20 parents arrive within 20 minutes, calls begin pouring in to the office, and students ask to go home.

Resource D

Outline of the Minimum Components of School Crisis Guidelines

The following is a sample *outline* of the minimum suggested components of a school crisis guideline document, which was discussed in Chapter 7. This outline is provided only to serve as a discussion item for further developing guidelines in the categories listed and/or in other areas unique to individual district and school needs. See Chapter 7 and the other chapters listed for clarification of any specific sections of this outline.

I. Definitions
   A. Board policy and/or position statement
   B. Definition of what constitutes a school crisis
   C. Crisis criteria
   D. Crisis levels

II. Response to Potential Crisis Situations
   A. Evacuation and lockdown procedures
   B. Noncriminal "What if?" situations
      1. Accidents with a large number of injuries, such as a school bus accident, airplane crash, or other mass catastrophe
      2. Death, serious illness, or other medical situations involving students or staff
      3. Environmental issues, such as hazardous materials release, chemical spills, or toxic waste
      4. Fire or explosions (such as a boiler explosion)
      5. Utility-related situations, such as a gas leak, or a power or water outage
      6. Student or adult demonstrations or protests, which might translate into criminal situations
      7. Weather-related situations, such as tornadoes, severe storms, floods, hurricanes, earthquakes, or other area-specific possibilities
   C. Criminal "What If?" situations

1. Abductions, such as kidnapping or noncustodial parent abductions of children
2. Altercations or riots, including large-scale fights, racially motivated conflicts, and gang-related disruptions
3. Bomb threats or suspicious devices
4. A drug overdose by multiple individuals
5. Gunfire in the school or on school grounds
6. Hostage situations
7. Terroristic threats, such as an Anthrax scare
8. Trespassers, suspicious persons, or "intruders"
9. Weapons possession, threats, and use
10. Violations of other laws and ordinances

III. Roles and Responsibilities
(See Chapter 8 for examples and details.)

IV. Crisis Communications Guidelines
(See Chapter 9 for details.)
   A. Internal audiences
   B. External audiences
   C. Media
   D. Others
   E. Agency and individual contact numbers, directories, and so forth

V. Mental Health Support for Grief and Healing

VI. Other District- and School-Specific Information
   A. Floor plans or maps
   B. Other information

References

Band, S. R., and Harpold, J. A. (1999, September). School violence. *FBI Law Enforcement Bulletin, 68*(9), 9-16. Washington, DC: Federal Bureau of Investigation.

Dwyer, K., Osher, D., and Warger, C. (1998). *Early warning, timely response: A guide to safe schools.* Washington, DC: U.S. Department of Education.

ESEA: School safety: Hearings before the U.S. Senate Committee on Health, Education, Labor, and Pensions. 106th Cong., 1st Sess. (1999, May 6). (Testimony of Kenneth Trump). Available on the World Wide Web: *http://www.senate.gov/~labor/hearingsrings/mayhear/050699wt/050699wt.htm*
and *http://www.schoolsecurity.org/news/senate.html*

Federal Emergency Management Agency. (1995, November). *Incident command system self-study unit.* Jessup, MD: Author.

Freedom Forum. (1998). Jonesboro: Were the media fair? [Online article]. New York, NY: Freedom Forum Media Studies Center. Retrieved May 24, 1999, from the World Wide Web: *http://www.freedomforum.org/newsstand/reports/jonesboro/printjonesboro.asp*

Goldstein, A. P. (1999). *Low level aggression: First steps on the ladder to violence.* Champaign, IL: Research Press.

Indiana Department of Education. (1999). *Checklist for a safe and secure school environment.* Indianapolis, IN: Author.

Johnson, K. (1993). *School crisis management: A hands-on guide to training crisis response teams.* Alameda, CA: Hunter House.

Johnson, K., Casey, D., Ertl, B., Everly, G. S., Jr., and Mitchell, J. T. (1999). *School crisis response: A CISM perspective.* Ellicott City, MD: The International Critical Incident Stress Foundation.

Kaufman, R., Saltzman, M., Anderson, C., Carr, N., Pfeil, M. P., Armistead, L., and Kleinz, K. (1999, August). Managing the unmanageable: Crisis lessons from the Columbine tragedy. *NSPRA Bonus* [Bulletin]. Rockville, MD: National School Public Relations Association.

Poland, S., and McCormick, J. (1999). *Coping with crisis: Lessons learned.* Longmont, CO: Sopris West.

Reed, S. (1999). Introduction. *Checklist for a safe and secure school environment.* Indianapolis: Indiana Department of Education.

Reisman, W. (1998, June). *The Memphis conference: Suggestions for preventing and dealing with student initiated violence.* Indianola, IA: Author.

Riley, R. W., and Reno, J. (1998). [Cover letter]. In K. Dwyer, D. Osher, and C. Warger, *Early warning, timely response: A guide to safe schools.* Washington, DC: U.S. Department of Education.

Silver, J. M., and Yudofsky, S. (1992). Violence and aggression. In F. I. Kass, J. M. Oldham, H. Pardes, and L. Morris (Eds.), *The Columbia University College of Physicians and Surgeons complete home guide to mental health* (pp. 385-393). New York: Henry Holt.

Steele, B. (1999, July). Guidelines for covering hostage-taking crises, prison uprisings, terrorist actions [Online article]. St. Petersburg, FL: The Poynter Institute for Media Studies. Retrieved March 17, 1999, from the World Wide Web: *http://www.poynter.org/dj/tips/ethics/guidelines.htm.*

Steele, W. (1998). *Trauma debriefing for schools and agencies.* Grosse Pointe Wood, MI: Institute for Trauma and Loss in Children.

Tompkins, A. (1999, April 30). After Littleton: Covering what comes next [Online article]. St. Petersburg, FL: The Poynter Institute for Media Studies. Retrieved March 17, 1999, from the World Wide Web: *http://www.poynter.org/research/lm/lm_afterlittle.htm*

Trump, K. S. (1998). *Practical school security: Basic guidelines for safe and secure schools.* Thousand Oaks, CA: Corwin.

U.S. Department of Education. (1999, August). Expulsions of students who brought guns to school drops significantly [Press release]. Washington, DC: Author. Retrieved November 18, 1999, from the World Wide Web: *http://www.ed.gov/PressReleases/08-1999/expulsion.html*

Recommended Resources

Dwyer, K., Osher, D., and Warger, C. (1998). *Early warning, timely response: A guide to safe schools.* Washington, DC: U.S. Department of Education.

Goldstein, A. P. (1999). *Low level aggression: First steps on the ladder to violence.* Champaign, IL: Research Press.

Johnson, K. (1993). *School crisis management: A hands-on guide to training crisis response teams.* Alameda, CA: Hunter House.

Johnson, K., Casey, D., Ertl, B., Everly, G. S., Jr., and Mitchell, J. T. (1999). *School crisis response: A CISM perspective.* Ellicott City, MD: International Critical Incident Stress Foundation.

Poland, S., and McCormick, J. (1999). *Coping with crisis: Lessons learned.* Longmont, CO: Sopris West.

Steele, W. (1998). *Trauma debriefing for schools and agencies.* Grosse Pointe Wood, MI: Institute for Trauma and Loss in Children.

CORWIN
PRESS

The Corwin Press logo—a raven striding across an open book—represents the happy union of courage and learning. We are a professional-level publisher of books and journals for K-12 educators, and we are committed to creating and providing resources that embody these qualities. Corwin's motto is "Success for All Learners."